The Politics of School Management

Eric Hoyle

HODDER AND STOUGHTON
LONDON SYDNEY AUCKLAND TORONTO

Acknowledgments

The author and publishers are grateful to the following for permission to reproduce material in this book:
The Athlone Press Limited for Table 1 (pp. 12–13); The British Educational Management and Administration Society for Table 2 (pp. 32–3); Basil Blackwell for Figure 4 (p. 104).

To Dorothy

British Library Cataloguing in Publication Data

Hoyle, Eric
   The politics of school management.—
   (Studies in teaching and learning)
   1. School management and organization—
   Great Britain
   I. Title   II. Series
   371.2'00941   LB2901

ISBN 0 340 38993 1

First published 1986

Copyright © 1986 Eric Hoyle
All rights reserved. No part of this publication may be reproduced or transmitted in any form or by any means, electronic or mechanical, including photocopy, recording, or any information storage and retrieval system, without permission in writing from the publisher or under licence from the Copyright Licensing Agency Limited. Further details of such licences (for reprographic reproduction) may be obtained from the Copyright Licensing Agency Limited, 7 Ridgemount Street, London WC1E 7AE.

Typeset by
Macmillan India Ltd, Bangalore

Printed in Great Britain for
Hodder and Stoughton Educational,
a division of Hodder and Stoughton Ltd,
Mill Road, Dunton Green, Sevenoaks, Kent,
by Richard Clay (The Chaucer Press) Ltd,
Bungay, Suffolk

Contents

Studies in Teaching and Learning		iv
1	Understanding Schools as Organisations	1
2	The Structural Looseness of Schools	22
3	Organisational Pathos and the School	51
4	Powerful Heads and Professional Teachers	73
5	Leadership and Mission	101
6	The Micropolitics of Schools	125
7	The School as a Thicket of Symbols	150
8	Conclusion	169
Bibliography		172
Index		185

Studies in Teaching and Learning

The purpose of this series of short books on education is to make available readable, up-to-date views on educational issues and controversies. Its aim will be to provide teachers and students (and perhaps parents and governors) with a series of books which will introduce those educational topics which any intelligent and professional educationist ought to be familiar with. One of the criticisms levelled against 'teacher-education' is that there is so little agreement about what ground should be covered in courses at various levels; one assumption behind this series of texts is that there is a common core of knowledge and skills that all teachers need to be aware of, and the series is designed to map out this territory.

Although the major intention of the series is to provide general coverage, each volume will consist of more than a review of the relevant literature; the individual authors will be encouraged to give their own personal interpretation of the field and the way it is developing.

1 Understanding Schools as Organisations

> Man is an animal suspended in webs of significance he himself has spun.
>
> CLIFFORD GEERTZ *The Interpretation of Culture*

Schools are organisations. Organisations differ from groups, families, communes, tribes and classes in having relatively specific goals, differentiated tasks, a clear division of labour, a structure for coordinating diverse activities, legitimate authority invested in certain members and a set of management procedures. There is no single organisation theory. The term is used to cover a diversity of perspectives, models and theories proper by which social scientists seek to understand organisations. Organisation theory is theory-for-understanding. We can thus make a broad distinction between *organisation theory* and *management theory*, which is practical theory and hence has a narrower focus. However, the distinction cannot be pressed too hard since management theory is grounded in, and the research which it generates contributes to, organisation theory. On the other hand, organisation theories frequently display a tendency to be normative and at least to contain an implicit commitment to improving life in organisations.

Organisation theory has a number of intellectual origins (see Burrell and Morgan, 1979), but there occurred a confluence of these different traditions in the 1950s and 1960s. There was much optimism at that time that if not a single theory then a dominant cluster of interrelated theories would emerge. This happened to some extent, though as we shall see, the consensus was challenged by competing perspectives from the mid-1970s onwards. However, although mainstream organisation theory contributed to an improved understanding of certain kinds of organisation, particularly industrial, commercial and public service organisations, it created less understanding of other kinds of organisation than had been anticipated. There was considerable optimism in the 1960s that organisation theory would enhance our understanding of schools (Hoyle, 1965). This optimism was misplaced. Recent reviews of contributions have been marked by a degree of despondency. Tyler (1982) writes: 'Schools seem to be particularly unsatisfactory subjects for sociological analysis. The attempt to perceive structure, wholeness and integrity in a school is fraught with so much difficulty that sociologists appear at best to fall back on metaphors.' Davies (1982) writes: 'It is rather like having several jigsaws, all with pieces missing, distributed in a number of boxes.'

However, one need not be too pessimistic. The difficulties encountered in seeking to apply organisation theory to schools have led to developments in organisation theory itself. The concept of organisations as loosely-coupled systems, a valuable development of the tight-coupling assumptions of bureaucracy, has owed much to the study of schools. Moreover, organisation theory *has* enhanced our understanding of certain aspects of schools, particularly those centring on authority, autonomy, professionality and decision-making.

The remainder of this chapter reviews some of the main approaches to understanding schools as organisations. This will provide a context for the remainder of the book. It will also illustrate why one must distinguish between understanding schools and understanding schools-as-organisations, since the latter approach is, as noted, limited and has far less power than other perspectives to illuminate the actual *process* of schooling.

The components of the school

One of the fundamental problems of organisational analysis is that of parts and wholes. Generally speaking, organisation theory tends to treat organisations as wholes, as entities, about which generalisations can be made. Educationists as well as social scientists frequently make the same assumption in two ways. One is to generalise about 'the school' as a type of organisation as in the statement: 'The school has become much more open to outside influence.' The other is to generalise about types of school by stating that 'A is a traditional school' or 'B is an open school'.

Parents, too, make generalisations about schools as entities, e.g. 'X is a good school' and actually make decisions about their children's schooling on this assumption of 'entitiness'. But schools are organisations which by definition are differentiated and have a number of parts or components. Thus to make generalisations about schools as entities is to make certain assumptions about the relationship between their parts and the whole. However, before discussing the problems inherent in these assumptions we can list some of the major components of the school:

Management: The structures and procedures involved in coordinating the diverse activities of the school.

Structure of tasks: The timetable, pattern of pupil grouping, organisation of pastoral care, etc. by which the transmission of knowledge and skill, the socialisation of pupils are structured.

Curriculum: The sets of knowledge, skills and values selected from a wider range and codified through syllabuses, schemes of work, etc.

Pedagogy: The process by which knowledge and skills are transmitted through class teaching and through informal processes of teaching and learning.

Informal structure: The unplanned patterns of association between teachers, between pupils, and between teachers and pupils.

Schools also have qualities which transcend their structures which are variously termed *cultures* or *climates*. Central to the concept of *culture* is the idea of *value*, that which is regarded as worthwhile by members of some group. These values are manifest in the norms which govern behaviour and the symbols – language, actions, artefacts – which express these values. Thus in a school with an academic culture there will be norms which emphasise academic endeavour perhaps symbolised through dress, honours boards, staff qualifications, etc. However, we have a part-whole problem here since distinctive subcultures develop amongst pupils which can have values quite opposed to the dominant culture of the school. *Climate* refers to the ways in which members of the school respond to that membership. It is essentially concerned with the quality of relationships between pupils, between pupils and teachers, between teachers, and between the head and teachers. However, these four sets of relationships are usually studied independently of each other. *Culture* and *climate* are to some extent terms for the same phenomenon but they are treated separately here since each has different theoretical and methodological roots and the relationship between them is far from clear.

Having listed some of the major components of the school we are in a position to point to what are perhaps the two fundamental issues to which organisation theorists must constantly address themselves. The first is the relationship between *structures* and *people*. The components listed above are 'depopulated' abstractions, yet organisations are essentially *people*. Thus the question of the impact of structures *on* people and the creation of structures *by* people is a perennial issue in the study of organisations. The second is the relationship between the components themselves. These have been listed separately above, but this is simply a device since it is clear that they are interrelated. The question is how far they and in what ways they are interrelated and whether their interrelationships are such that one can treat a school as an entity, as a system. We can explore these issues further.

Structure and people

All organisations have essentially three interrelated components: people, structures and resources. If we first consider the dimensions of people and structure, a well-known model conceived by Getzels and Guba (1957) is a valuable guide. The basic model is thus:

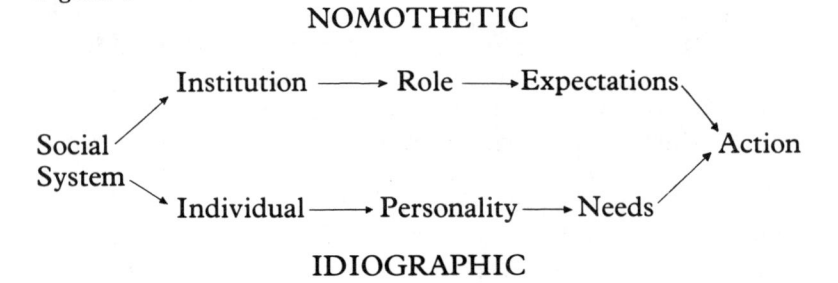

Figure 1

NOMOTHETIC

Social System → Institution → Role → Expectations ↘
                                                    Action
            ↘ Individual → Personality → Needs ↗

IDIOGRAPHIC

The basic assumption is that social systems have two main components, the nature of the interaction between which determines their collective actions or outcomes. The top dimension on the model refers to structure. It is termed *nomothetic* because it is the more predictable and rule-governed dimension. Its components are successively defined as one moves from left to right. *Institutions* are the regular, patterned activities of the system or organisation. In the case of the school these include teaching and learning, pastoral care, pupil selection and differentiation, etc. On this model these institutions are defined in terms of the *roles* of the members of the organisation. In the case of the school these include the academic, pastoral and administrative roles of teachers and the academic and age-related roles of pupils. In role-theory, roles are defined by the *expectations* attached to them. Thus the expectations attached to the roles of head and most junior French teacher will differ considerably. The nomothetic dimension, then, is formal, patterned, relatively enduring and can be conceptualised independently of people; the role structure remains relatively stable whilst different incumbents of the roles come and go. The nomothetic dimension of the school is expressed in terms of timetable, the class pattern of the primary school, the academic departmental structure at the secondary school and, also in the secondary school, the pastoral structure of houses, year groups, etc.

The other dimension brings in *people*. It is termed *idiographic* because it represents the unpredictable, idiosyncratic and particular qualities brought to the organisation by those who 'people' it at any point in time. Again the components become more specific as one moves from left to right. *Individuals* are defined by their *personalities* which, in this model, are defined by their *needs*. Thus although structures pre-exist individuals, since even in a new school these are determined to some degree by external factors such as LEA policies or general expectations about how schools should be internally structured, and hence are to some degree a constraint on individuals, the idiosyncratic characteristics of those who become members of the school will shape, modify or lead to a reinterpretation of the structures. This can be readily seen in the relationship between *role* and *personality*. The teacher's role is shaped by individual personalities, but expectations attached to the role limit the degree to which the role can be re-shaped. The head who takes coffee in the staff room is not treated, even in that informal context, as would be another teacher. Conversations between teachers and head, though relaxed, are likely to retain a greater degree of formality than conversations between teachers of equal status.

A third element of the school as an organisation, i.e. *process*, represents the interplay between these two components. Getzels and Guba insert the following line between the two already given:

$$\text{group} \longrightarrow \text{interaction} \longrightarrow \text{climate}$$

but although this usefully indicates the place of group behaviour in mediating between structures and people, it does not so readily convey the daily processes of classroom interaction, staff decision-making, peer group resistance to rules, etc. It is this process which is the real stuff of school life.

A question thus arises about the 'reality' of the nomothetic dimension. The 'objective' elements of organisations are buildings, equipment and people. The 'structures' which constitute the nomothetic dimension are, in practice, people coming together on a regular, institutionalised basis. That is what we can *see*: teachers and pupils in classes, teachers in meetings and so forth. As we noted above, these structures can be represented in timetables, etc. but it is people who make them 'work', especially people with power.

Essentially there are two approaches to this theoretical problem. One is to treat structures *as if* they were real and relatively independent. This is what we will discuss below as the *systems perspective*. Two things follow from this. One is that in some ways organisations can be studied and compared independently of those who 'people' them at a particular time. Thus one could make a study of, say, decision-making structures or pupil-grouping quite independently of whoever happened to be the head, the teachers or the pupils. This is what is essentially happening when studies 'demonstrate' that mixed ability teaching is more effective than streaming. Adherents to another view, to be discussed below as the *phenomenological perspective*, treat structures as having no existence outside human consciousness and thus concentrate their attention on the ways in which they are socially constructed.

The systems perspective

This is the perspective which underpins most organisation theory. Its basic assumption is that organisations have clear boundaries within which there are a number of subsystems, having different functions in relation to the whole. These subsystems have a sufficient degree of integration to ensure that the system just survives and, beyond that, achieves to some degree the ends which the system has been created to pursue. Moreover, since each system is part of a larger system, it will receive inputs from this larger system which will then be transformed in some way to emerge as outputs into this larger system. The most fundamental form is *general systems theory* which can be applied to an organisation, a human body, a flock of birds or a candle flame.

General system theory was initially generated by biologists and physiologists and there is an obvious analogy with a human organism and its components of brain, heart, liver, kidneys, etc. which have to remain within a measure of interdependence if the organism as a whole is to stay healthy. The organism can survive various forms of illness, for which the organisational analogy would be forms of conflict, and indeed can survive and remain reasonably effective despite the removal of organs which have, in any case, no positive function, e.g. the appendix, and even some which have. Systems theory suggests that a change in one part of this system will stimulate changes in other parts of the system in order to restore equilibrium, the process of *homeostasis*. A final point which can be made is that systems can have different ways of achieving the same end product. In systems language this is *equifinality*.

General systems theory is given particular form according to the phenomena under consideration. We have above given some hint of its biological application though this is put in a highly simplistic form. Systems approaches underlie much work in engineering. There is also an approach termed *socio-technical systems theory* which is concerned with the relationship between work groups and technology, and there is *social systems theory* which has wide application in the social sciences including the conceptualisation of organisations as systems (see Buckley, 1967). For the purpose of the present brief discussion we can divide systems theories into three categories: the 'strong' systems approach, the 'loose' systems approach and the 'conflict' view.

We can do no better to indicate the nature of a strong systems view than quote Louis and Sieber, (1979):

1   An organisation, and the individuals who are members, behave as if the organisation had relatively stable goals.
2   The goals of an organisation are specified or elaborated by management groups.
3   For an organisation to function effectively, there must be consensus between organisational members on operational goals, particularly on the strategic tasks of the organisation and how they are to be performed. Where there is no consensus, the tasks will not be adequately performed and conflict will ensue.
4   Subordinates within an organisation must, under most circumstances, remain compliant to the task definition which is set out by their superiors. If they are not compliant, conflict will occur.
5   The organisation can tolerate little conflict in the operational goals of its subgroups, and there is a need for conflict to be rooted out and resolved.

There are elements in this strong system view which are prima facie attractive to those who attempt to understand schools as organisations. The key concepts of the strong system approach are *goals, functions, consensus* and *socialisation*. Each type of organisation is held to have certain goals. It has to be said that this brief account of the *structural functionalist* variant of systems theory is simplified to the point of caricature and the interested reader should consult the key works of Talcott Parsons for a powerful and elegant systems theory in relation to all social systems (Parsons, 1951) and educational systems in particular (Parsons, 1966). The application of Parsons' systems theory to schools is discussed by Hills, 1968, 1976; Dreeben 1968, 1976.

Armed with such a theory the individual studying an organisation can attempt to judge the functionality of its various components in relation to its goals and, moreover, to determine what structures and processes are dysfunctional. For example, we take it as axiomatic that the basic structure of primary schools is unspecialised class teaching whilst that of secondary schools is specialised teaching. Parsons (1959) would argue that this is so because the major function of primary schools is socialisation and that this requires a sustained relationship between teachers and pupils whilst the major functions of secondary schools are the transmission of specialised knowledge and the differentiation of pupils in anticipation of their prospective occupational roles. However, the strong systems view has been heavily criticised from within the systems tradition by those who adopt a 'conflict' position and by phenomenological sociologists. These criticisms will be discussed in the next section.

The 'loose' systems approach does no more than accept the concept of system as a heuristic device for exploring and explaining the characteristics of organisations. Clear goals, high consensus and tight integration are not taken as axiomatic. The protagonists of loose systems models simply use a systems framework as a heuristic for exploring the presence, or absence, of integration between the different components of an organisation. The functionalists' stress on commitment to goals, integration, consensus and adaptation disappears as a theoretical commitment but the questions remain and are approached in a less dogmatic way on the basis of empirical research. In his well-known paper on schools as loosely-coupled systems Weick (1976) states that his use of the term 'system' was deliberate since however loose the coupling there remains a systematic relationship between components.

This brings us to the third systems perspective which we can term the 'conflict' approach. The basic assumptions of this approach are the reverse of the 'strong' systems or functionalist position. Whereas functionalists perceive social systems as characterised by value consensus, solidarity, cooperation, integration and the acceptance of legitimate authority, conflict theorists perceive social life as based on conflicting interests which can only be resolved by the coercion of those without power by those with power or through inducements of various kinds, and then only temporarily since social systems are inherently unstable.

It may seem perverse to some readers to include conflict theory under the heading of the systems perspective since it is at such odds with the 'strong', structural functionalist approach. However, it is included here because it is ultimately predicated on the assumption that organisations are systems with interrelated components, but stresses that these components are as likely to be in conflict as in a high degree of coordination and that ultimately conflict can become so acute that the system breaks down. Thus like other systems theories it is concerned with the capacity of an organisation to survive or not to survive (Gouldner, 1959).

The phenomenological perspective

In this section we can group together a number of perspectives, particularly symbolic interactionism, phenomenology and ethnomethodology, which, though differing from each other, share certain characteristics which constitute a radically different way of conceiving social reality from that of the protagonists of systems approach. The account is necessarily oversimplified and the interested reader should refer to Burrell and Morgan (1979).

The phenomenological approach gives priority to *people* and their *actions*. The social world essentially consists of people interacting with each other, negotiating patterns of relationship and constructing a view of the world. In the process of interaction different groups come to see the world differently, to develop different concepts of reality, and to construct different bodies of knowledge. However, although the process of interaction, negotiation and reality-construction are continuous, the outcomes become institutionalised and although continuing to undergo change as a result of individual and group interaction, develop a relative degree of permanence. Thus economy, politics, education and all the other major social institutions, and their constituent organisations, develop an apparent degree of independence through their roles, their procedures and their structures. But essentially they are nothing other than *people* and the *ideas* which have been socially constructed. Thus institutions and organisations have no objectivity beyond human consciousness, they are not 'out there', and their structures should not be 'reified', i.e. treated as if they had a reality independent of people. The economy of social life makes it necessary for people to carry these constructs in their minds but their only reality is the subjective reality created in the process of social life. Greenfield, a leading protagonist of a phenomenological approach to organisations and their management, has summarised the position thus:

> We may better understand organisations if we conceive them as being an invented reality, an illusion that rests on a kind of social sleight-of-hand. It is true that organisations appear to be solid, real entities that act independently of human control and are difficult to change. Yet the paradox is that the vital spark, the dynamic of organisation is made from nothing more substantial than people doing and thinking. Organisations are limited by and defined by human action. In their deepest-subjective reality, they are simply manifestations of mind and will. While this conception of organisations does not make them easy to control or to change, it does locate organisational reality in the concreteness of individual action. (Greenfield, 1980).

In a strict sense there can be no phenomenological theory of organisations since the concept of organisation assumes that at least it refers to a social unit which has some degree of 'entitiness' about which objective statements can, in principle, be made. For the phenomenologist, there can be no single organisation but only a set of compelling constructs. The school which the headteacher speaks of on speech night is not necessarily the school which the teachers present would recognise, and is less likely to be a school which the pupils present recognise. The school is conceptualised differently by different sets of participants. They construct a reality out of their interests. If there happens to be a commonality of perspective and hence a construct shared by all members, this arises from the fortuitous fact that their interests are held in common, or that those with power in the organisation have succeeded in socialising the lower participants into an acceptance of their own view. The concerns of the phenomenologist, therefore, are the interactions between members and the realities which they construct. They are interested in the processes at work within an organisation rather than with their alleged structures. Thus the strengths of a phenomenological perspective have been seen in the contexts of classroom and peer group interaction rather than in organisations as such. On the other hand, the symbolic interactionist approach, though treating the social world as a social construct, is prepared to attribute sufficient stability to undertake at least tentative comparative generalisations between organisations as such.

Systems and phenomenological perspectives contrasted

We can do no better than to quote the distinctions made by Greenfield (1975).

Table 1 Alternative bases for interpreting social reality (from Greenfield, T. B. (1975) 'Theory about organizations: its implications for schools' in Hughes, M. (ed.) *Administering Education: International Challenge*, The Athlone Press)

WHAT IS SOCIAL REALITY?

Dimensions of comparison	A natural system	Human invention
Philosophical basis	Realism: the world exists and is knowable as it really is. Organisations are real entities with a life of their own.	Idealism: the world exists but different people construe it in very different ways. Organisations are invented social reality.
The role of social science	Discovering the universal laws of society and human conduct within it.	Discovering how different people interpret the world in which they live.
Basic units of social reality	The collectivity: society or organisations.	Individuals acting singly or together.
Method of understanding	Identifying conditions or relationships which permit the collectivity to exist. Conceiving what these conditions and relationships are.	Interpretations of the subjective meanings which individuals place upon their action. Discovering the subjective rules for such action.
Theory	A rational edifice built by scientists to explain human behaviour.	Sets of meanings which people use to make sense of their world and behaviour within it.
Research	Experimental or quasi: experimental validation of theory.	The search for meaningful relationships and the discovery of their consequences for action.

Table 1 (Continued.)

Dimensions of comparison	A natural system	Human invention
Methodology	Abstraction of reality, especially through mathematical models and quantitative analysis.	The representation of reality for purposes of comparison. Analysis of language and meaning.
Society	Ordered. Governed by a uniform set of values and made possible only by those values.	Conflicted. Governed by the values of people with access to power.
Organisations	Goal-oriented. Independent of people. Instruments of order in society serving both society and the individual.	Dependent upon people and their goals. Instruments of power which some people control and can use to attain ends which seem good to them.
Organisational pathologies	Organisations get out of kilter with social values and individual needs.	Given diverse human ends, there is always conflict among people acting to pursue them.
Prescription for curing organisational ills	Change the structure of the organisation to meet social values and individual needs.	Find out what values are embodied in organisational action and whose they are. Change the people or change their values if you can.

The epistemological assumptions underpinning the two perspectives are probably irreconcilable. The social theories which are expressed in each are incompatible at the extremes but possibly not in the more moderate versions of each. The potentially common ground is that the phenomenological account of the constructions of social reality and hence social institutions is essentially correct. Solutions to human problems are constructed on the basis of social interaction and common understandings. If the solutions are successful they become institutionalised as the various practices in education, religion, law, politics, economics and the family. These institutions come to be seen as if they *are* objective, permanent and functional, although it is clear that they are always undergoing constant minor and many major changes. The secondary school is an institution, but changes are constantly occurring in particular secondary schools as a result of redefinitions of the situation by teachers and pupils, and of policy changes at local and national levels. The articulation between these levels is extremely difficult to establish since it is so complex and to a large degree adventitious. This micro-macro linkage is the perennial problem of the social sciences. The extreme functionalist variant of systems theory treats those institutions which have persevered over time as immutably functional and hence there is the problem of accounting for change since all innovations are thus to be interpreted as dysfunctional. The phenomenologist, on the other hand, is an extreme relativist, sees the world as being in a constant process of re-definition, and hence challenges the existence of the reified institution of the functionalists. The intermediate position is to accept that institutions *are* socially constructed and *are* to some degree functional in relation to their place and time, but are amenable to change and are, in fact, constantly undergoing change, although their fundamental characteristics change only slowly. Thus marriage is a social institution but its nature varies over place and time and undergoes change. Likewise the distinction between primary and secondary education exists in many societies because this would appear to meet the needs of those societies but it would be dangerous to affirm that the primary and secondary distinction is immutably functional. The intermediate position between the two extremes can reconcile the two perspectives in broad terms, but the concerns of the two positions are different. The systems approach tends to be concerned with persistence, regularity, order and at least a limited degree of functionality, whilst recognising that the institutions and organisations studied are only relatively stable. The phenomenologist is less concerned with structures than with processes involved at the microcosmic level as groups construct new realities within the framework of relatively enduring institutions. Thus the difference becomes one of choice of problems and methods since, as the present writer has noted elsewhere, one cannot look down both ends of a telescope at the same time.

Understanding schooling, understanding schools

There is a certain irony in the expressed disappointment about the contribution of organisation theory to our understanding of schools. On the one hand, students of a school as a *type* of organisation have made an important contribution to organisation theory through the concept of the loosely-coupled system. On the other hand, many students of schools have made unwarranted assumptions about the tight relationship between their components and particularly about the predominant influence of the formal structure. The perspective adopted in these latter studies has been that of testing theories of organisation, often theories generated within an industrial context. However, the best studies of schools have either adjured tight theory or have focused on substantive problems rather than structures.

Understanding schools as organisations is not to be equated with understanding the process of schooling. The latter is perhaps best understood through studies of the curriculum, classroom interaction and of the relationship between them of which there are many excellent British studies. Another profitable area of study has been the structure and culture of pupil peer groups and how these have related to the process of schooling. Here again some investigations have reported their relative independence of formal structure (Lambert, Bullock and Millham, 1973), although there is evidence of a relationship between one aspect of structure, streaming, and the values held by peer groups. The best British studies of schools and schooling have focused on the process of pupil differentiation: by grouping, by curriculum, by teacher labelling, by peer-group membership, etc. (for example, Hargreaves, 1967; King, 1969, 1973; Lacey, 1970; Ford, 1969; Woods, 1979; Ball, 1980). Thus, in relation to the dimensions of the school listed above, these studies have been concerned mainly with aspects of the structure of tasks, curriculum, pedagogy, informal relationships and culture. They have not been concerned with the managerial dimension and, with the exception of King's use of Weber as a resource, they have made little use of conventional organisation theory. In contrast, a large number of American studies of schools have been concerned with the managerial domain. At the present time, there is little to suggest that there is a systematic relationship between the managerial domain and the core task dimension of teaching and learning. The only hint of this comes from studies of climate which suggest that the relationships between heads and teachers, which are the basis of the administrative climate, are related to the relationship between teachers and pupils (Revans, 1965). The well-known study of Rutter *et al.* (1979) relates the ethos of the school and effectiveness and suggests a relationship between ethos and leadership, though the styles and strategies of the heads remained outside the scope of the research.

One form of criticism of organisation theory holds that the process of schooling cannot be understood by reference to the characteristics of schools as organisations but by reference to the social, political and economic characteristics of society (see Bell, 1980). The Marxist view of education tends to perceive the process of schooling as corresponding to the structure of society (for example Bowles and Gintis, 1976). A study of Mapledean, an English primary school, by Sharp and Green (1976), seeks to relate the classroom activities of teachers to the social, political and economic character of capitalism. The school as such is not treated as a factor. This view also treats the management dimension of schools as a reflection of political forces in society. Schools are perceived as arenas in which political conflicts are enacted. It has been a principle of the New Left that schools and other institutions should be politicised as part of the process of transforming sociey, the 'long march through the institutions'.

Holistic models of organisation

In spite of the difficulties entailed in conceptualising organisations, including schools, as entities, organisational theorists of all persuasions utilise holistic models. Each model conceptualises the organisation in a different way by focusing on one aspect of its complexity. Some examples are:

1. *Organisation as structure* (a) This is the most common model in organisation theory and much employed in research on industrial organisations. Structures of activities and their management are taken as the key independent variables with other components explained in relation to

these. This takes many forms ranging from the tight functionalist model to the loose-coupled system model.
2 *Organisation as structure (b)* Unfortunately the term *structure* is used to refer to very different models and the relationship between the two concepts is far from clear. This second, far less widely used concept, draws on linguistic and anthropological structuralism to identify the relationship between components. Sociologically its roots are in Durkheim rather than Weber and its key protagonist in education is Bernstein who developed his views partly as a reaction to what he saw as the superficial and simplistic application of organisation theory to schools. His focus is on the deep structure of the curriculum which varies between strong and weak forms of *classification* and *framing* (see Bernstein, 1975; Gibson, 1977; Tyler, 1983; King, 1976, 1981).
3 *Organisation as social system* Again this term has different connotations. It is a basic functionalist concept but is also widely used to conceptualise an organisation as a network of social relationships, though sometimes, in relation to the school, this is confined to social networks amongst pupils (Gordon, 1957; Coleman, 1961).
4 *Organisation as socio-technical system* This is essentially a variant of organisation-as-structure (a). It focuses on the interaction between structure, technology and social relations (Miller and Rice, 1967; Woodward, 1972). It would appear to have little relevance to the school which makes comparatively low use of technology. However, if one conceptualises technology broadly and does not confine it to hardware, this approach can be used to generate a number of important issues, particularly the persistence of class teaching when the means for a resource-based approach to teaching and learning are to hand.
5 *Organisation as symbol system* This model treats structures as relatively stable patterns of interaction which are based on a process of interpretation by organisational members. The organisation, though having ostensibly 'real' formal structures, is essentially the outcome of negotiation amongst members.
6 *Organisation as theatre* This is a variant of the organisation-as-symbol system which focuses on its drama-

turgical aspect with members perceived as playing roles according to scripts for which meetings and other encounters are the settings (Mangham, 1978, 1979).

7 *Organisation as social construct* Although there cannot strictly be a phenomenological theory of organisation since this perspective denies the possibility of the objective reality of an organisation which can be understood by an outside observer, participants can nevertheless have a concept of the organisation as an entity and a subjective experience of what it means to be a participant in such an organisation. This concept is amenable to study through interpretive techniques which rely mainly on the analysis of language, observation and open-ended interviews. For discussions about this approach, and a critique, see Greenfield (1975), Gronn (1983).

8 *Organisation as political system* Here the key organising concept is that of *interest*. Organisational members are conceptualised as political actors strategically using various resources of power in pursuit of individual or group interests.

9 *Organisation as economic system* Microeconomic theories of the firm are applicable to industrial organisations but hardly to schools. Nevertheless there have been some attempts within the economics of education to apply input-output models for schools and apply economic principles of cost effectiveness.

This brief list of models of organisations which are in use by no means exhausts the possibilities. There are variations within each model and numerous combinations. The reader should consult Burrell and Morgan (1979) for a different and more complex typology of perspectives on organisation. Burrell and Morgan include in their typology radical organisation theories and even anti-organisation theories which challenge the very existence of certain kinds of organisation. The best-known protagonist in education is Illich (1971).

There is no 'right way' to understand organisations. Each model has a different focus and thus approaches the problem from a different perspective. Thus each model, each theory, each methodology has its strengths and limitations. The same set of events is amenable to different explanation depending on the model, such as Allison's classic study of the Cuban missile crisis illustrates (1981).

Studies of schools as organisations

It is impossible to review this substantial field of study in a brief section. Fuller accounts have recently been given by Davies (1982) and King (1983). This section will therefore be limited to making a number of points about empirical studies of organisation.

A variety of research methodologies are available to the student of schools as organisations, and various choices have to be made. One can make a broad distinction between studies *of* organisations and studies *in* organisations. The first takes the organisation as such as a framework. Of course, it is not possible to capture all the complex interactions of an entire school within a single framework, but studies of schools as organisations yield insights into the character of the school as such. The second type of study is concerned with relationships between two or three organisational characteristics, e.g. pupil grouping and achievement, leadership style and teacher satisfaction (Hoyle, 1973).

Almost inevitably perhaps, the best studies of schools as organisations have been case studies of single schools or perhaps of two schools. Although many such studies, particularly American, have been informed by organisation theory, they have not been theory-testing studies but studies which set out to observe a school as such, or a specific aspect such as innovation, authority or climate, or a particular substantive problem, for example, Clark (1960), Smith and Keith (1971), Gross, Giacquinta and Bernstein (1971), Swidler (1979).

As noted above, many of the best British studies have hardly relied upon organisation theory at all but have been observational studies of aspects of schooling. One of the few case studies of the management component of a British school is that of Richardson (1973). There are fewer comparative studies of schools (for example King, 1973; Rutter *et al.*, 1979). One of the difficulties involved in comparative studies is that they are either labour-intensive, if observation is involved, or limited in the nature and amount of data which can be collected by means of questionnaires.

An attractive approach to the study of organisation in our present state of knowledge is the *development* of theory rather than the *testing* of theory. This has been advocated by Glaser and Strauss (1967) who propose as an alternative to the strict testing of theory the building up of theory through what they term the 'method of continuous comparison'. This involves the building on the insights obtained through the study of one organisation by pursuing these in other organisations in different contexts. Thus insights attained from a case study of a comprehensive school might be explored in other comprehensive schools perhaps of different size, with an ostensibly different form of internal structure or a different social context, or in other kinds of school: primary, independent, approved schools, etc. This grounded theory approach is popular amongst MPhil and PhD students, but very few such students are able to devote their careers to the method of continuous comparison which would be essential to the building up of theory.

It has been conceded that for a number of reasons, the contribution of organisation theory to the understanding of schools has been disappointing. However, the case *for* organisation theory is that it enhances our understanding of the management component and, to a lesser extent, structure of tasks component of schools and that it provides a loose organising framework for a variety of studies of schools. This is to accept a systems model, at least a loose systems model, since it assumes some relationships between components. Without being too sanguine about the relationships which might be established, the issues enhanced in these relationships are of the greatest importance, since they turn on the effectiveness of schools as organisations. The view that 'schools don't make a difference' emerged in the United States in the 1960s as a result of large-scale studies, particularly that of Coleman (1966), which were interpreted as showing that the 'output' of the schools (i.e. pupil achievements) could be predicted by their 'inputs' (i.e. pupil characteristics and various kinds of resource). On the other hand, there are a number of studies which suggest that dimensions of schools, the structure of activities and climate in particular, *do* seem to make a difference in terms of pupil advancements (Brimer *et al.*, 1977; Power, 1967; Reynolds and Sullivan, 1979).

The evidence to hand at the present time suggests an hourglass model of the school with the top section containing the management dimension and the bottom section contains the 'schooling' dimension.Studies such as those of Rutter *et al.* (1979) at least suggest a relationship between the two which, like the hole in the hourglass, could be vital. The organisation-theory-as-framework approach would see relationships as being established on the top and bottom compartments of the hourglass and possibly, between the two elements.

The scope of this book

The concerns of this book are very much to be seen as being within the top compartment of the hourglass. The issues dealt with are mainly centred in the management dimension and, to a lesser degree, the structure of activities dimension. Its concerns are limited to one small part of the school system. It is not, for example, concerned with the teaching and learning process and not at all with pupils. The approach is theoretically eclectic. To some extent the book is grounded in conventional organisation theory, but it also seeks to utilise a number of emerging perspectives which stress the political and symbolic aspects of organisations. Its purpose is not to present a definitive account of how the school, or one approach to school management 'works'. We do not yet know enough to be definitive on that. Its purpose is to encourage readers to think about a number of issues relating particularly to power and professionality in schools.

2 The Structural Looseness of Schools

> The beginning of administrative wisdom is the awareness that there is no one optimum type of management system
>
> BURNS AND STALKER *The Management of Innovation*

Schools are not battalions, nor are they communes. Battalions are tightly coordinated, tasks are clearly specified, rules are detailed and enforced through clear disciplinary procedures, orders are transmitted down an unequivocal chain of command, and much time is committed to the process of coordination. Communes are loosely coordinated, tasks are dffuse, rules are minimal and there is much emphasis on shared values as the basis of integration. On a simple continuum of tight versus loose integration, schools would be located somewhere between the two. However, within and between types of school, some will incline more towards one pattern of coordination whilst others will incline towards its opposite.

Schools are characterised by what has been termed a *structural looseness* (Bidwell, 1965) and fall into a category of organisations whose internal structures and links with their environment are *loosely-coupled* (Weick, 1976). These terms convey the fact that although schools have rules and procedures for coordinating their internal activities, they are also marked by a high degree of autonomy enjoyed by the various components: individual teachers, departments and pastoral units. The purpose of this chapter is to explore some aspects of this structural looseness and particularly the relationship between organisational patterns which incline either towards the tight or loose structuring of the school. (See Willower, 1982, for a discussion of the loose-coupling notion in relation to schools.)

A working distinction which will enhance the argument of this chapter is between *coordination* and *integration*. *Coordination* will be used to refer to those interrelationships between the units and tasks of the school which are the outcome of deliberate actions on the part of the head or the management team. *Integration* will be used in a broader sense to embrace coordination plus other sources of interrelationship which include internal and unplanned patterns and also, at a deeper level, the relationships which are inherent in the curriculum and pedagogy of the school. Another useful working distinction is between the *prime tasks* and the *support tasks* of schools. *Prime tasks* are those which are concerned with the education of children and include teaching and pastoral work. *Support tasks* are those tasks, largely administrative, the purpose of which is to facilitate the process of teaching and learning.

There is a permanent tension between *prime tasks* and *support tasks*. As this distinction is formulated, the latter are subservient to the former but for a number of reasons, e.g. the expectation that the school should manifest *order*, the imperialism of heads, the waywardness of some teachers, the perennial problem of pupil control, and day-to-day contingencies, they interpenetrate so much that the distinction is tenable only in the broadest of terms and only at a conceptual level. Nevertheless, the distinction is an important one since a major concern of organisational theorists is to establish an appropriate balance which will ensure efficient coordination whilst not detracting from the prime tasks of the school.

Patterns of coordination

The concept of *bureaucracy* is an inevitable starting point for any consideration of patterns of coordination. Schools are *not* bureaucracies, although they may have bureaucratic elements, yet this concept must be the point of departure for four reasons. Firstly, it has been a powerful and persistent model of organisation. Secondly, it is the model with which others are compared and contrasted. Thirdly, bureaucracy has been the model which has most frequently been operationalised in research on organisations. And fourthly, bureaucracy is a term, almost invariably a term of disparagement, used in everyday discourse. The concept of bureaucracy has its origins in the work of Max Weber (1947). Weber perceived that the functions of modern industrialised societies would be increasingly fulfilled through complex organisations and he postulated an ideal type to encapsulate the key features of patterns of coordination in organisations of all kinds. An *ideal type*, it should be pointed out, is not 'ideal' in any moral sense; it is 'ideal' in the Platonic sense of an abstract form against which actual manifestations can be compared. Thus bureaucracy would be rarely found in its pure form but most organisations approximate to this model to some degree. It is a heuristic device rather than a description of reality.

Weber discussed bureaucracy at a number of points and Pugh *et al.* (1976) claim that twenty-six different dimensions are to be found in Weber's writings. However, the following are the dimensions most frequently included in the model:

hierarchy
specialisation
centralisation
procedural rules
impersonality
authority of office.

In a truly bureaucratic organisation, goals would be determined by those legally empowered to do so; the means to the achievement of these goals would be specified and codified; they would be passed down a hierarchy of technically-competent personnel who would ensure the impersonal application of rules. Thus the ideal type bureaucracy is, in theory, fool-proof. If everyone 'went by the book' then nothing would go wrong. It should be said, however, that Weber did not personally find bureaucracy a cheerful prospect. He applied to it the tag: *sine ira et studio* ('without hatred or passion and hence without affection or enthusiasm', Weber, 1947).

Of course, hardly was Weber's ink dry when the critics of his model began to have their say: Could bureaucrats be trusted to establish organisational goals in a democratic society? Were not rule-following members of organisations robbed of their dignity? Where was the scope for creativity? Would not impersonality be inimical to motivation and commitment? Does a single hierarchy fail to take account of the contribution of professionals? These objections and many more were levelled at the concept of bureaucracy. In a well-known paper, Merton (1958) outlined the *bureaucratic personality type*, the desiccated *apparatchik* whose sensibilities and creativity become stultified through years of operating the system. The layman fulminates against bureaucracy because he perceives it as a system concerned with *preventing* him from achieving his ends by creating procedural obstacles often involving paperwork—the French term for bureaucracy is *la paparassie* and the British equivalent is 'red tape', the Treasury tape tied around civil service papers.

An excellent account of bureaucracy is given by Berger, Berger and Kellner (1974). They identify three central components of bureaucracy. These are: *competence* ('Each jurisdiction and each agency within it is competent *only* for its assigned sphere of life and is supposed to have expert knowledge appropriate to this sphere'), *proper procedure* ('Bureaucracy is assumed to operate within national rules and sequences') with the concomitant possibility of improper procedures and hence avenues of redress, and *anonymity* ('Bureaucratic competences, procedures, rights and duties are *not* attached to concrete individuals *but* to holders and clients of bureaucratic officers'). They also identify the following components of the cognitive style of bureaucracy: *orderliness* (i.e. a system of categories into which everything within a certain jurisdiction can fit), *general and autonomous organisability* (i.e. the principle that everything is potentially organisable), *predictability* (i.e. because procedures are known all is predictable), a *general expectation of justice* (i.e. everyone in the relevant category will receive equal treatment), and *moralised anonymity* (i.e. the system is deemed to have moral obligations to its clientele the members of which may be anonymous). Using another idiom, there is a 'hidden curriculum' inherent in bureaucracy. It is not simply a set of procedures for accomplishing certain specified ends, but the procedures themselves are infused with a certain moral tone.

The above distillation of the key elements of bureaucracy appear to be more characteristic of bureaucracy at an institutional rather than an organisational level and, indeed, Berger, Berger and Kellner take as their example a government agency, specifically one concerned with the issue of passports. Bureaucracy may well take a different form at the organisational level. However, whilst the principles of bureaucracy thus depicted would appear to invite the opprobium of many, there are elements which might attract general support. On this account bureaucracy has the virtue of order, security, justice and predictability.

Thus bureaucracy is not, contrary to popular usage, wholly despicable. One has here a situation where a sociological concept has become part of everyday speech and as such has a particular pejorative connotation whilst remaining a sociological concept which is value free. In organisational analysis, the concept is used as a starting point for theoretical formulations but is also operationalised as a basis for the empirical study of organisations. There are basically two different approaches to the operationalisation of the concept. One is to develop direct measures of organisational properties, e.g. levels of hierarchy, extent of specialisation, degree of centralisation. The other is to develop a questionnaire, one of the best known of which is that devised by Hall (1963), designed to determine members' *perceptions* of the extent of bureaucracy in their organisations. The scores of respondents are then summed to yield an index of perceived bureaucracy in a particular organisation which is then used comparatively to establish the incidence of perceived bureaucracy in organisations of the same and of different types, and as a measure to correlate with other variables, e.g. size, innovativeness, morale, effectiveness.

Bureaucracy is the predominant model of tight control within the sociological tradition. It is the model with which all sociological students of organisation have to engage and it has been said, without too much exaggeration, that all sociological organisation theory is a footnote to Weber. However, similar models involving tight control have had a parallel existence in management theory. They have their origins in the work of the time and motion pioneer, F. M. Taylor. This 'classical' model was developed particularly in relation to industrial organisations with a clear production goal whereas bureaucracy was perhaps more orientated towards public service organisations. However, the work of Mayo (1933) and his associates Roethlisberger and Dickson (1939) showed that insofar as classical management models were predicated upon the notion of 'economic man' who would accept any working conditions which would maximise his earnings, they were misguided since the more appropriate concept was 'social man' for whom the social context of work ranked high or, on a later formulation, 'self-actualising man' who sought to fulfil his expressive needs through his work. From these studies stemmed a new tradition which focused on questions of motivation and the integration of individual and organisational needs. This led to the formulation of models of organisation other than the bureaucratic. Hence an alternative model to unnecessarily tight control has emerged.

The model has stemmed largely from the work of management theorists. The most frequently used label is *human relations* but a variety of other terms have been used, e.g. *organismic* (Burns and Stalker, 1961), *Theory Y* (McGregor, 1960), *participative* (Likert, 1961) and *organic-adaptive* (Bennis, 1966). These different terms have emerged because there are divergencies between the models due to the different emphases given to particular elements. However, in spite of the different nuances between these theorists, and some minor contradictions between elements, the underlying models have a number of elements in common. Perhaps the most fundamental is the emphasis on *integration* rather than *coordination.* Another fundamental component is the strong humanistic assumption that individuals should be sufficiently free from external constraints to enable them to develop their capacities to their highest level. The model entails a minimisation of rules, hierarchy, detailed job specification and departmental boundaries. It entails a maximisation of collaboration, creativity, adaptiveness of structures to problems to be solved, and participative decision-making.

The differences between the models will not be explored in detail here and the reader is referred for more extensive consideration to one of the standard works on organisation theory (e.g. Perrow, 1972a). However, it should be pointed out here that the human relations model in the view of its protagonists is a theory of management which combines humanism and efficiency. Its domain is essentially industrial and as such contains a number of contradictions when applied to the school. Perhaps the most crucial of these is the inherent incompatability between integration and autonomy. However, this will be considered in some detail later in the chapter.

Schools as bureaucracies

Like all summary concepts, *bureaucracy* can be highly illuminating. It has been so widely used by sociologists that the term has become virtually universal because it succeeds in capturing the experience of coping with organisations. However, it can, if pressed into service as the dominant model of organisational coordination, serve to mislead. Three points can be made about the application of the concept of bureaucracy to schools. The first point is that in terms of empirical research the concept of bureaucracy 'works'. In other words, when some measure of bureaucracy is applied to schools it can be shown that schools differ significantly in their degree of bureaucratisation and that bureaucracy correlates fairly well with other measures. Research on schools has normally taken the form of inviting teachers to complete a questionnaire on their perceptions of their schools as bureaucracies. The problem here is that the questionnaire imposes the sociologist's 'second order construct' since teachers are forced to respond within the framework of the questionnaire, whereas the 'first order constructs' which teachers use to make sense of the world, their everyday language, may not include the concept of bureaucracy. Moreover, to focus on bureaucracy means that the investigator cannot focus on alternative ways of conceptualising the school. Katz (1964), emphasising the structural looseness of schools, argued that a different picture would emerge if *autonomy* was taken as the key concept. It is inevitable that sociologists will find only what their concepts and methods are directed towards. Different studies might find the same school as characterised both by bureaucracy *and* autonomy. In practice, schools *are* a mixture of the two. Nevertheless, the use of bureaucracy as a concept has generated a number of interesting studies within that framework. One of the most extensive was Anderson's (1968) study of teachers' perceptions of bureaucracy in a large metropolitan district in the United States which demonstrated school differences and also positive correlations between bureaucracy and other variables such as school size, social class background of pupils, and sex ratios on school staffs.

The second point is that bureaucracy is not a unitary concept. Although there is general agreement on the major components of bureaucracy as an ideal type, these components may not necessarily cluster together in any particular organisation or type of organisation. Thus bureaucracy is relative in two senses: the degree of bureaucracy can vary between all the components considered together or between individual components. An interesting study was carried out by Punch (1969) in eight elementary schools in Ontario. Using a modified version of Hall's (1963) scale he explored six central dimensions of bureaucratic structure: (1) hierarchy of authority; (2) specialisation; (3) rules for incumbents; (4) procedural specifications; (5) impersonality; and (6) technical competence. He found that four of these dimensions, those numbered (1), (3), (4) and (5) above, correlated highly and constituted a distinct bureaucratic factor. The two other dimensions, (2) and (6), correlated highly with each other but not with the other four, thus constituting a second factor which Punch regarded as a 'professional' factor. This is an interesting finding but it is perhaps important to draw a distinction between what one might call routine and non-routine specialisation. The former would refer to the specialisation of the assembly line where each worker has a single specialised task. The latter would refer to professional specialisation where, though limited in the range of activities involved in the task, the expertise involved ensures a degree of autonomy. Subject teachers in a secondary school would experience this specialist teaching as enhancing their freedom to make professional judgments since others do not have the expertise to control the teacher's work. The complexity of the relationship between the different elements of the bureaucratic model has been shown by the Aston studies of management in industrial settings (Pugh and Hinings, 1976). In particular, the relationship between centralisation and specialisation is problematic. Moreover, some of the relationships between bureaucracy and other variables which one might hypothesise have not been supported in studies of schools. For example, Moeller and Charters (1966), in their study of the relationship between bureaucracy and teachers' sense of power in school districts (not individual schools it should be noted) in the United States, found that the higher the degree of bureaucracy the *greater* the teachers' sense of power. Heward (1975), in a study carried out in a sample of secondary schools in the Midlands using a modified Aston scale, found that bureaucratic structure and innovation were positively correlated. Packwood (1977) has argued that hierarchy remains a potentially valuable pattern of coordination in schools which can recognise, nurture and respond to members' needs.

The third point is that one should perhaps make a distinction between bureaucracy as *structure* and bureaucracy as *style*. Some elements of bureaucracy are inherent in organisational structures or, at least, imposed on organisations by outside forces. Hierarchy, for example, is inevitable in schools since it is determined by the structure of the Burnham scale. But other elements of bureaucracy vary according to administrative style.

Coordination in all organisations is dependent upon the observation of rules. Thus all organisations are to some degree bureaucratic in this sense, but the number and detail of the rules laid down by the head will determine the degree to which a school is perceived as bureaucratic. Moreover, some ways of doing things may be more bureaucratic than others. Who could doubt, for example, that the teachers in the boys' secondary modern school to whom the following notice was issued would be likely to interpret its very tone as bureaucratic?

Figure 2

SOME GENERAL NOTES

1. **Registration** –(a) *Control.* Every boy must sit still and in absolute silence.
    (b) *Present.* RED diagonal, herring-bone pattern.
    (c) *Absent.* BLACK O to fill space.
    (d) *Totals.* Count number of boys before entering total.
    (e) *Late Arrivals.* Send with form-captain to Secretary.
    (f) *Mistakes.* Do not alter registers in any way. Send note with form-captain to Secretary.

2. **Canteen Registers.** All entries must be in *ink.*
    (a) *Monday payments* in RED INK. *Total* at bottom.
    (b) *Present and absent* as in class register.
    (c) *Daily totals* — total, paid, free. (Do not advertise free meals.) Count the show of hands.
    (d) *Late payments* in BLACK on day of payment.
    (e) *Credits* — allow credits as shown.
    (f) *Requests for free meals* — refer all queries to Secretary.
    (g) *Master* — daily mark. RED DIAGONAL or BLACK O or D or S.

3. **Mark Books**
    (a) Enter names.
    (b) Get marks for every boy quickly.

4. **Record of Work Done**
    (a) Keep regularly and carefully.
    (b) Keep records at school.

5. **Reward and Punishment**
    (a) *Rewards*: (i) House points.
    (ii) *Work shown* on notice-board.
    (iii) *Boy's work* reported to Head by master i/c.

Figure 2 (Continued)

(b) *Punishments*:
- (i) *Official detention* — only for lateness and other breaches of school discipline; *not for class discipline.*
- (ii) *Keeping in.* Master i/c may keep boys behind after school. Ask if he is due for Official Detention. If he is, send note of name and form to Master i/c detention. **NB** *4.30 pm* is latest time for detention or keeping in.
- (iii) *Impositions.* Give only useful copying-out of your own work. Insist on good writing in ink, to time, properly set-out, correct number of lines, etc.
- (iv) *Standing out.* A class offender may be stood at the BACK of the class facing the wall. NEVER IN FRONT. NEVER OUTSIDE THE ROOM.
- (v) *Sending to Head.* Only in emergency with a note and an escort. The escort must return with news of arrival and reception. Master i/c must report to Head at the first break afterwards.

6. **Boys out of class**
   (a) *Toilet.* Discourage boys from going in class-time — certainly not immediately after or before a break.
   (b) *Exemption-slip* must be produced for any absence from class.
   (c) *Boy unwell.* Should sit at back of class; or, if serious, sent under escort with a note to Head. *Never send a boy home.*

7. **Sending Messages.** Never verbally, always in writing.

8. **Smoking.** Only in staff-room.

Considerable care needs to be exercised in attributing bureaucratic properties to schools. The primary school has relatively few bureaucratic properties, but can be administered in a bureaucratic *style*. Grammar schools, likewise, have few characteristics of bureaucracy. Their coordination was based on a *traditional* authority (Weber, 1947) and value consensus. The key feature of these schools is their structural looseness. Where the educational process is largely a matter of relatively autonomous classroom teaching, the need for coordination is relatively low and bureaucracy is minimised. As schools become larger they become more bureaucratic in the sense of having more coordinating activities, but a counter-trend is at work since size permits a greater freedom of sub-units from central control. Herriott and Firestone (1984) found that primary schools were more bureaucratic than the more loosely-coupled secondary schools.

Non-bureaucratic patterns of organisation in schools

The following table distinguishes between some characteristics of bureaucracy and its alternatives (Hoyle, 1976b):

Table 2

Dimension	Model A	Model B
Role	*High specificity* Duties carefully specified. Expectations rigid. Little scope for the free play of personality. (School) The teacher's role is prescribed by specialism, class unit and place in the hierarchy.	*Low specificity* Considerable flexibility in how the role is enacted. Scope for spontaneity and creativity. (School) Teachers have scope to play a set of variations on their role vis-à-vis pupils and colleagues. They can step out of their specialisms if necessary.
Rules	*Detailed* Actions controlled by 'the book'. (School) Teachers must follow specific procedures in teaching and in the general administration of the school.	*Alternative or diffuse* Rules kept to a minimum. General rather than detailed, giving the individual scope to interpret them in the light of circumstances. (School) Teachers assumed to have their own educational goals and to pursue these with a minimum of rule-following behaviour. The general rules interpreted in the light of educational goals, and 'bent' if necessary.

Table 2 (Continued)

Dimension	Model A	Model B
Structure	*Rigid* Strong boundaries between components. (School) Rigid timetabling, pupil grouping, curriculum divisions.	*Flexible* Permeable boundaries between components. (School) Flexible timetabling, grouping and curriculum divisions.
Authority	*Hierarchical* Authority based upon 'office' and orders passed down through the hierarchy. Supported by legal sanctions. (School) High degree of authority vested in the head and transmitted through heads of departments, etc.	*Collegial* Authority located in the groups of professional equals who govern their affairs by democratic procedures. Influence rather than sanctions. Expertise rather than power. (School) School policy decided by an academic board in which all teachers participate on a democratic basis.

Changes in schools in the 1960s were in the direction of Model B, not necessarily from an extreme form of model A, but from an intermediate model in which central authority and teacher autonomy were intermingled. The pressure towards Model B stemmed from a variety of sources. Undoubtedly, schools were influenced by the socio-political trends whereby it was believed that those who would be affected by decisions should have a greater opportunity to participate in the decision-making process itself. As courses in educational management expanded during the same period, headteachers became exposed to human relations theories of management whereby participative decision-making structures were held to facilitate more widespread decision-making and greater responsibility amongst those who would otherwise be at the bottom of the hierarchy, and enhanced self-actualisation, motivation and hence commitment. However, another trend peculiar to education led to many schools moving to a Model B kind of organisation with developments within the curriculum which entailed concomitant changes in school structure, relationships between teachers and professional authority. We can focus on the last of these trends using Bernstein's work as a resource.

Bernstein's approach owes more to Durkheim rather than to Weber. It is concerned with fundamental patterns of social integration and his work is essentially structuralist in that it is focused on relationships between the components of a text or text analogue such as a unit of behaviour, an organisation, a curriculum or any distinctive coherent and internally-integrated unit (see Taylor, 1979; Gibson, 1984). In his initial article on this theme, written partly as a critical response to the approach from organisation theory, Bernstein (1967) argued that changes in the basis of social integration in society generally were likely to be reflected in the structure of the school. In short, schools would become more 'open' as the boundaries which constituted their structures were eroded or became more permeable. Thus to a greater degree the school would be socially constructed and re-constructed through negotiation between members. Subsequent papers focused on the curriculum rather than on school organisation, but the concepts employed were concerned with the 'deep structure' of the school which underpinned both. These concepts were *classification*, i.e. the principle governing relationships between components of the curriculum, which could be *strong* or *weak*, and *frame*, i.e. the principle governing the pedagogical relationship, which again could be *strong* or *weak* (Bernstein, 1971). He is careful to stress that he is concerned with the principles which govern the *relationships* between elements rather than their contents. As an aside, it can be said that it is difficult to 'place' Bernstein in relation to the competing phenomenological and the systems perspectives. He argued (Bernstein, 1975) that his approach combines both: *classification* representing the limiting structure and *framing* representing the possibilities of action. However, this would need further elaboration than has been so far given to these terms in this context.

At the end of the 1960s the present writer, informed by an article by Bernstein (1967), sought to identify some of the directions of change which would appear to have been occurring over the preceding decade on ten dimensions (Hoyle, 1974). These were as shown in Table 3.

The model can be elaborated to include many more dimensions, but will suffice for our present purpose. Janowitz (1969)

Table 3

Dimension	From	To
Curriculum Content	Monodisciplinary	Interdisciplinary
Pedagogy	Didactic teaching	Discovery learning
Organisation of Teaching/Learning	Rigid timetabling	Flexible timetabling
Pupil Grouping	Homogeneous	Heterogeneous
Pupil Choice	Limited	Extensive
Assessment	Single mode	Multiple modes
Basis of Pupil Control	Positional	Personal
Teacher Roles	Independent	Interdependent
School-Community Links	Low	High
Architecture	Cellular plan	Open plan

outlined a distinction between *specialisation* and *aggregation* models which have some similarities with the one given as the 'dilemmas' facing education identified by Berlack and Berlack (1981).

The question is whether the changes were unrelated and adventitious or the manifestation of a fundamental change in the deep structure of schooling. Such structuralist questions are inevitably somewhat abstract, but if there is a fundamental difference in the organising principle, the key concept is perhaps that of *boundary*. The difference between the 'closed' model and the 'open' model is that the former has strong boundaries between components and the latter weak boundaries, as Bernstein suggested. In the 'open' model, compared with the closed model, there is an erosion or increased permeability of boundaries: between curriculum components, teachers and taught, pupil categories, teachers' tasks, teaching groups, divisions of the school day, the physical dimensions within the school building, school and community.

It is difficult to assess how far schools have moved towards Model B. There is little doubt that many schools made some changes to some extent along some of the dimensions. However, it is likely that there was more written and talked about innovation than implementation and Peter Wilby, a knowledgeable and astute educational journalist, has written about 'the revolution that never was'. King (1976, 1981) sought to test Bernstein's model through a re-analysis of existing data and the collection of new data and discovered very little shift in pedagogy. However, the principles with which Bernstein was concerned are particularly difficult to operationalise. Tyler (1983) reports a methodological enquiry into the conceptual adequacy of Bernstein's codes. But whereas King's work tested the coherence of the surface features of the code, Tyler conceptualises them in deep structural terms, formulates a statistical analogue and, in the absence of the necessary data for schools, uses the data from the Aston studies of organisational structure to establish the validity of the analogue and thus, indirectly, establish support for Bernstein's codes. It has to be said that this analysis shows the codes to be far more complex, and more interpenetrative than the simplified bipolar model which is the basis of the above discussion.

The 'closed' characteristics of openness

The loosely-coupled nature of school implies in Lortie's term (1969) a 'balance between autonomy and control'. The head plays a key role in determining the direction of the school and establishing appropriate procedures. On the other hand, teachers have a relatively high degree of classroom autonomy in relation to what is taught, but particularly in the matter of how it is taught. In secondary schools, relatively autonomous departments stand intermediate between the central administration and the class teacher. It is assumed by those who see the loose-coupling as functional that the prime task of the school is carried out by teachers in their classes but that the supportive tasks which facilitate teaching nevertheless involve a degree of central coordination. The 'dysfunction' of bureaucracy occurs when the supportive tasks impinge on and distort the prime task. The 'open' school clearly conforms to the human relations model outlined above. In terms of the process of schooling it is predicated on the basic assumption of progressive education that children will be more highly motivated where they have a degree of control over their own learning. It assumes that teachers likewise will flourish as creative pedagogues when they are free to create their own roles and create their own structures in collaboration with colleagues. 'Open' schools present an alternative to bureaucracy, but as such they are confronted with

THE STRUCTURAL LOOSENESS OF SCHOOLS

two dangers, the Scylla of chaos and the Charybdis of close control by peers. Both undermine the loose-coupling of schools.

'Chaos' is a charge frequently made by unthinking critics against innovative schools, but although this is a manifest overreaction, the problem of coordination cannot be summarily dismissed. The loosely-coupled school provides a structure, a mesh within the spaces of which the prime task can be carried out. An 'open' school implies a making of the boundaries which constitute the mesh and the danger is that a school can, to adopt terms which Richard Peters used in a different connection, move from a 'mesh' to a 'mush'. Bernstein (1975) pointed out that in open schools 'problems of boundary, continuity, order and ambivalence' are likely to arise.

The evidence from the case studies of 'open' schools illustrates the intransigence of this problem. A structure essentially consists of rules. Order in 'open' schools is dependent upon external rules being replaced by internalised norms and a constant process of negotiation. Both are dependent upon group acceptance of a particular view of schooling by teachers and pupils, but the socialising power of the school has frequently been overestimated.

The internalisation of norms as an alternative to external imposition of rules is dependent upon a high degree of consensus amongst a school staff and thus dissent presents serious problems. Creating consensus involves a great deal of time and can divert effort from the prime task of teaching. Case studies of such schools indicate that staff become involved in interminable discussions in trying to construct an agreed mission for the school. Another problem is that the collaborativeness which is implicit in the open-school model can be achieved only at the expense of teacher autonomy. Collaboration at the level of policy making, planning and pedagogy winkles the teacher out of the traditional insulated, isolated autonomous classroom role. In discussing the prospects for team-teaching, Lortie (1964) notes that collaboration in teams makes the teacher much more accessible to peer control. Although bureaucracy is a highly controlling pattern of coordination, there are limits to its pervasiveness and the teacher can ensure a degree of privacy and choice. This privacy is lost where peer control is dominant. Since autonomy is an important element in teacher's job satisfaction (Jackson, 1968), the open school pattern can constitute a threat to this. There is thus an irony in the fact that innovations in school structure and control, stimulated in part by a wish to provide an alternative to the perceived tight control over both teachers and pupils as manifest in some existing patterns, have resulted in a loss of at least the *individual* autonomy which was available to the teacher within the mesh of a loosely-coupled system.

However, because there is no single human relations model the term can be used to describe situations in which entire organisations are integrated through close, interdependent relationships and others where there is high integration of a human relations kind *within* components: departments, teams, etc., but these components are relatively independent of each other. Burns and Stalker's (1961) *organismic* model and Bennis's (1966) *adaptive systems* model are of the latter kind. As such, they conform rather more to the model of a *loosely-coupled system* which we can now consider.

Schools as loosely-coupled systems

As a matter of observation and report, schools are neither highly coordinated through bureaucracy nor highly integrated through a school-wide human relations approach. They conform to the loosely-coupled systems model. This was pointed out in one of the earliest and most penetrating reviews of the school as an organisation (Bidwell, 1965) which noted the *structural looseness* of the school. Lortie's (1969) discussion of 'the balance between autonomy and control' expressed the same idea. However, the term 'loosely-coupled system' became widely adopted following Weick's article (1976). He writes: 'By loose-coupling, the author intends to convey the image that coupled events are responsive, *but* that each event preserves its own identity and some evidence of its physical or logical separateness.' However, he remarks that he will use the term 'loosely-coupled *system*' since he wishes to emphasise that sets of elements persist across time, presumably because they have, despite their 'looseness', system-like properties.

Weick observes that schools are loosely-coupled systems. Moreover, although he notes the strengths and weaknesses of loose-coupling, the not-so-implicit message of his paper is that for the school the advantages of loose-coupling outweigh the disadvantages. We can summarise his discussion of strengths and weaknesses in the following table:

Table 4

Advantages	Disadvantages
1 Fosters the perseverance of the organisation by enabling it to respond to environmental changes	Archaic traditions are perpetuated
2 Sensitivity to changes in the environment	Vulnerability to responses and interpretations
3 Potential for localised adaptations	Loss of the advantages of standardisation
4 Potential for generating novel solutions in the separate parts	Though novel solutions may be generated, lack of linkage prevents their diffusion
5 Breakdowns in one part of the systems are readily 'sealed off' preventing a spread to other parts	Poor inability to 'repair' the defective parts because they remain isolated
6 The possibility of high autonomy for actors e.g. teachers	Autonomy entails the separate response to a problem when established procedures or a collective response could be adapted
7 Relative inexpensiveness following from low coordination costs	Non-rational allocation of funds which are therefore unspecifiable unmodifiable and incapable of being used as a means for change.

Litwak (1961) published a paper on 'models of bureaucracy which permit conflict' which contrasted the *bureaucratic* and *human relations* models and proposed a third, the *professional* model, which combined elements of each. His argument was that *bureaucracy* best meets the needs of organisations facing routine tasks and the *human relations* approach the needs of organisations facing unpredictable and hence non-routine tasks. For organisations facing both routine and non-routine tasks the *professional* model is held to be appropriate. This model provides a structure within which the professional has sufficient freedom to function effectively. Litwak and Meyer (1965, 1974) discuss the administrative structures of schools arising from their work on school-community linkages in the Detroit Great

Cities Project. They developed what, in fact, was a loosely-coupled systems model in which they described, and implicitly prescribed, the *professional* or, in later terminology *compartmentalised*, system for the school. This model had the following components:

1 Hierarchical *and* collegial authority structures.
2 Generalisation *and* specialisation amongst staff.
3 Both personalised *and* impersonalised social relationships.
4 Both a priori rules *and* internalised goals.
5 Both an integration of policy and administration (defined here as implementation of policy) in certain contexts *and* their separation in others.
6 The presence of internal mechanisms of isolation which exist in *neither* the bureaucratic nor the human relations mode.
7 Appointment on merit (the only element common to all three models).

In elaborating this model in relation to the school they write:

> More typical and more plausible is the supposition that educational and socialisation tasks of the public schools are both uniform and nonuniform. Not only are the housekeeping aspects of the school likely to be amenable to routine but certain educational aspects as well. Thus, scheduling and distribution of time to different subjects, some common evaluation standards, and even some teaching techniques may be conceived of as uniform tasks. In fact, some standard patterns emerge and new procedures and techniques may convert nonuniform into uniform tasks. On the other hand, schools must deal with problems of motivation and socialisation which are not uniform. The art of teaching and management of the school so as to facilitate education demand far more than science and technology can now make predictable and standard. This is the condition for which our analysis asserts the appropriateness of the compartmentalised administrative style. It permits rationalistic management of the routine components in the work of teachers and other persons in the organisation while providing a human relations style to operate with respect to nonuniform components. In a sense, this is the meaning of the assertion that the administrative style should allow the teacher in the school to act as a profession.

Litwak and Meyer discuss in some detail each of the components of their model except, strangely, that concerned with internal mechanisms of segregation which is probably related to the concept of loose-coupling. Litwak's (1961) paper cites some mechanisms of segregation, e.g. the physical segregation of those departments which would function more effectively if isolated from each other, but these examples are drawn from industrial rather than educational organisations. However, Litwak and Meyer (1974) discuss in considerable detail patterns of loose-coupling between the school and its community and thus provide a good illustration of the concept in this sphere.

The concept of loose-coupling underlines the point that in fact there are few instances of the purest form of either Model A or Model B schools, although there is no logical reason why schools cannot be structured according to the principles of Model A or integrated according to the principles of Model B. Thus most schools in fact and in general terms, conform to a model intermediate between Models A and B. We can call this Model C, but it must be stressed that the components of this model are not internally coherent. The configuration of the Model A and Model B elements will vary from school to school and over time within the same school. There are insufficient studies to indicate whether there are particular configurations which tend to occur. Perhaps what one can say is that the configurations in primary and secondary schools are likely to be systematically different. Tyler's description (1973) of the school as: 'a confederation of autonomous classrooms under the hegemony of the headmaster' is clearly more applicable to primary schools than to secondary schools, although even in primary schools this would be less true now than when Tyler made this point, since a number of factors have combined to modify the autonomous class-teaching pattern.

In the secondary school the loose-coupling will be much more diverse because there are more units than in a primary school: classes, tutor groups, academic departments, school divisions, pastoral units, etc. which may incorporate different, even conflicting, values; the loose-coupling between the 'academic' and 'pastoral' sides of schools has often been remarked upon in the literature.

A theoretical formulation of the principles of what we have here termed Model C has been attempted in an Open University Unit on the Urban School (Raynor *et al.*, 1974). The 'professional' model (i.e. Model C) is held to be associated with the following strategies:

Flexible grouping.
A mixture of teaching and cooperative learning.

Stress on the creation of talent.
Stress on intensive labour techniques: professionals, ancillaries, volunteers.
Individual and group achievement on the source of motivation.
Control of deviant behaviour through counselling, pastoral care and school-based social workers.

The model also links a number of institutional arrangements associated with the 'professional' form. As the context of this model is a unit on urban education it is not surprising that these are particularly related to the relationship between school and community. They are:

Education for social and community amelioration.
An adaptive curriculum based on social process and community needs.
A major stress on social experience starting with the local community.
The cultivation of diffuse community contacts with the entire staff involved.
Training and experience in community development and social action.

It must be stressed that this configuration is one set only from a potentially wide range of possibilities. It will be noted that although this particular configuration contains elements of Models A and B, it is much more like the latter than the former and emphasises a coupling which is more tightly than loosely integrated. It is reported here as one example of an attempt to work out a Model C configuration.

It is clear that the concept of loosely-coupled systems is employed not only descriptively but, for some kinds of organisations which would include schools, prescriptively. Thus organisational theory underpins the currently influential *contingency theory* of management. In their seminal study Burns and Stalker (1961) stated that 'the beginning of administrative wisdom is the awareness that there is no one optimum type of management system'. This view has increasingly informed management theory as the environments in which organisations have to function are becoming much more turbulent. Hanson and Brown's (1977) formulation of the assumption of contingency theory can be summarised as follows: Organisations are open-systems influenced by their environments and have overlapping goals. Whilst all organisations have universal problems they also face problems which are unique. Hence effective performance involves a match between external requirements and internal constraints. This has to be achieved in a context in which a manager can rarely take on problems from their outset and never knows all that is going on around him. Thus leadership style needs to vary with the problem. Structures need to be flexibly differentiated since different problems require different structures to handle them.

Contingency theory is widely discussed and associated research reported in relation to industrial organisations. Two of the major contributors to the field, Lawrence and Lorsch (1967), employ the key concepts of *differentiation* and *integration*. *Differentiation* is the sub-division of parts and *integration* refers to the interrelationship between the parts. Theirs is an open systems model and focuses on the functional relationship between internal structure and the demands of the environment. The balance between differentiation and integration has to be appropriately struck if the organisation is to be effective. In stable environments, and we must remember that as the theory was developed in relation to industrial organisations and therefore the key aspect of the environment is the market, organisations can be relatively undifferentiated but highly integrated. However, in dynamic environments more differentiation, which essentially means the capacity of the different parts to respond rapidly to environmental change, has to be accompanied by a sufficient degree of integration between the parts. Contingency theory has emerged as the synthesis of bureaucracy and human relations models, but it should again be noted that this does not imply that effective organisations are always found to have a mid-way mix of the two approaches. In some instances a highly bureaucratic structure can be effective, in others the human relations approach can be the more effective style. The 'mixed' model is functional where organisations confront routine and non-routine problems.

There is now a considerable literature on various aspects of contingency theory in relation to industrial organisations (see Burrell and Morgan, 1979, for a summary). However, there is rather less literature on contingency *management* theory, insofar as this can be distinguished from loose-coupling *organisation* theory, in relation to schools. Tyler's (1973) paper was an early attempt to explore the possible applications. Most empirical work has been undertaken in the United States. Derr and

Gabarro (1972), Hanson (1979b) and Hanson and Brown (1977) have explored the relevance of contingency theory to American schools or school districts and broadly speaking confirm that the most effective organisations are those which are able to sustain a contingency approach.

Experiments in open schools

Of necessity we have to use simple terms to convey complex social situations. The complexity is such that the term used may have the agreement of those who use it in professional discourse, but different participants will attach to it different meanings. This is very much the case with the term 'open'. It has been used so far in this chapter to indicate the removal of boundaries of the kind discussed elsewhere and thus equated somewhat with the human relations approach to organisation and management. The variant meanings of 'open' will only be elaborated in this section insofar as the distinctions are relevant to the argument, but one important point which can be made at the outset is that we should distinguish between 'open' schools and 'open' classrooms. In the 1950s and 1960s changes occurred in the primary school which were labelled 'progressive' and later as a move to 'openness'. For most primary schools, however, the openness operated at the classroom level as a result of the greater flexibility in terms of curriculum and pedagogy. In this section we are concerned with open *schools*. Summerhill is perhaps the best known of the open schools in the independent sector. A. S. Neill's ideas have been influential on some teachers in the public sector, particularly on those teachers who staffed the free schools which emerged in the 1960s to decline and virtually disappear in the 1970s. In the public sector many schools moved towards openness, some further than others. Those which travelled furthest in that direction tended to generate publicity, especially when they ran into difficulties.

The history of innovative schools in the public sector in both Britain and the United States has been somewhat mixed. Countesthorpe College in Leicestershire was innovative in design, in its approach to curriculum and pedagogy, and in its decision-making structures. The school faced a degree of parental and political hostility and experienced difficulties in sustaining its original mission. The first Warden, Tim McMullen, left after the fourth term but, against the expectations of many, an appointment was made of a new Warden, John Watts, who was committed to the same aims as Tim McMullen. The school withstood the criticism. An HMI inspection led to a report which was far less critical than many had anticipated, but which did imply that the school attempted too much too quickly. The school subsequently institutionalised many of the innovations under John Watt's leadership. (For the original Warden's approach see McMullen, 1968. For accounts of the early years of Countesthorpe see Bernbaum, 1973, Watts, 1977 and the materials produced as Case Study 5 of the Open University Course E 203, 1976.)

The case of William Tyndale Junior School in Islington is very different. The head and a number of members of staff were committed to a radical approach and a curriculum which was to be grounded in the everyday knowledge of the children from the predominantly working class catchment area. This was linked with a pedagogy in which pupil choice was a strong feature. This group rejected, in the words of one member, 'the late 1960s style of informal progressive repression' by which is meant, one assumes, innovations in learning which were confined to classrooms and which remained very much under the control of the teacher—Bernstein's 'strong framing' (see also Sharp and Green, 1975). This radical approach was opposed by other members of staff, one of whom became a vociferous critic. The school generated considerable publicity and opposition from parents, managers and others and the ILEA set up an enquiry under Robin Auld which was highly critical of the radical members of staff who were eventually dismissed. (See Auld, 1976 for a detailed report of the Enquiry, Gretton and Jackson, 1976 for an extended account of the affair, and Ellis et al., 1976 for the views of the dismissed teachers.)

Smith and Keith (1971) undertook an investigation of the first year of operation of Kensington, an American elementary school. Some of the features of Kensington reported by Smith and Keith are the following:

> The program was to capture team teaching with all of its varying organisational possibilities—ungradedness, total democratic pupil-teacher decision making, absence of curriculum guides, and a learner-centered environment. The idea to prevail was primarily that of freedom from staid educational means which, in turn, would

unleash both faculty and students from the difficulties of the traditional and move toward an individualised learning program.

Smith and Keith's analysis revealed what they termed 'social change out of control'. The 'grandeur' of the change strategy generated uncertainty amongst the teachers, unintended outcomes, a conflict between the pre-determined 'institutional plan' and democratic decision-making. There was community dissatisfaction about the school and Shelby, the first principal of the school, resigned in the first semester of the second year. Smith and Keith summarise the outcome as follows:

> A new organisation has a mandate, a charge as it were, and it has the special problems of getting started, that is, coming to terms with the several environments, building a social structure, and facing up to resource limits. An organisation with an innovative program complicates this process. In addition, the educational leaders of . . . Kensington had both a strategy and series of operational tactics, 'innovations facilitating innovations', for implementing the innovative program in the new organisation. The accent was on planned purposive social action. However, in our descriptions and interpretations, Kensington suggested the phenomenon of social change out of control. The potency of a functionally oriented systems theory kept reappearing.

Although there are some differences between Kensington and other innovative schools which have been reported to the literature, there is the essence of a general pattern in the sequence of events which suggest that where open patterns of schooling have been attempted some common difficulties have been encountered. Of course, it should be emphasised that there are probably many successful implementations of the innovations described which have not been the focus of research or publicity. However, it does appear that the open (or human relations) approach has often foundered and there are different accounts of why this has occurred.

The *political* account sees failure to sustain open schools as the result of conservative external pressures. It is a fact that in many of the reported cases there has been strong external resistance to the internal changes. The 'liberal' version holds that the examination system which ties school achievement to educational opportunities is the source of this external resistance. The 'radical' version shares this view but contextualises it in a broader political framework. New Left views prevalent in the 1960s saw open schools as an aspect of 'the long march through the institutions', the achievement of social change through the politicisation of institutions and organisations. The external pressures were thus seen as the capitalist hegemony reasserting itself. This view sees teachers as essentially conservative and, in some instances such as at William Tyndale, resisting changes directly within the school, or as liberals who, though seeking changes on 'educational grounds', were essentially concerned with liberalising the system rather than changing it radically and therefore unwilling to combat resistance. The genuine efforts at changes made by radical teachers are seen as being negated through criticism and even victimisation. The political account of change, especially in its radical version, represents a recognition of the limits of a phenomenological perspective. Although schools are social constructs and are thus amenable to reconstruction this 'possibilitarianism', as it has been called, is limited by the power of the political system (Whitty, 1974).

The *managerial* account holds that the failure to institutionalise open schools is due to the lack of an appropriate strategy of change. This is essentially the view taken by Gross *et al.* (1971) in their case study of Cambire, an American elementary school in which efforts to sustain innovations in curriculum and pedagogy were thwarted by the teachers' lack of clarity about the innovation, their lack of needed capabilities, the lack of appropriate teaching materials, the incompatability between the innovation and the structure of the school, and the low level of commitment of the staff. The literature on innovation suggests that it is likely to be successful when a problem-solving orientation within the school has been established through organisational development, where teachers are enabled to extend their professionality through school-focused professional development, and where the necessary external support is provided. The literature tends not to address itself directly to the question of piecemeal versus holistic change but assumes that teachers in a school will decide which strategy best meets their needs and competences. (See Schmuck and Miles, 1971; Havelock, 1973; Hoyle, 1970, 1973; Fullan, 1972; Schmuck *et al.*, 1977; Dalin, 1973; Whiteside, 1978; Bolam, 1974, 1982.)

The *functionalist* account is based on the assumptions that the most effective structure will depend upon the goals of the school. There are perhaps two variants of this. One is that open-schooling failed to become institutionalised because it lacked congruence with the goals which society has established for its schools. This view is, of course, compatible with the conservative and radical elements in the *political* account, the former approving the goals, the latter rejecting them. On this view, open-schooling would become a possibility if educational goals changed. The second variant of the functionalist account is that it emphasises contingency, the need for the school to oscillate between open and closed structures as changes in the external environment – political, economic, social and technical – lead to changes in educational goals and means. On this view, a degree of openness was functional in relation to the wider educational context of the 1960s, but radical openness failed because it was an over-adaptation. The third variant is that although superficial innovations can be successfully adopted, effective schools must also meet certain instructional imperatives, e.g. the class as a basic unit, teacher-directed learning, rules governing pupil behaviour.

Space does not permit a full analysis of the schools in terms of loose-coupling and contingency models. However, one can hypothesise that two particular problems would be encountered by these Model B schools. In some cases the schools were internally well-integrated on the basis of value consensus, but where these values were at odds with those of the environment there was a lack of relatively detailed subsystems which could cope with this problem. In other instances, although there was a notable absence of consensus within the school, the decisions were such that none could alone cope with a hostile environment. This underlines the point that loose-coupling, if it is to be effective, needs at least a minimum of systematic integration between the parts, hence Weick's insistence on using the term loosely coupled *system*.

It need not be emphasised that the above comments reinforce the radical criticism of systems theory as being essentially conservative. The underlying prescription is for an adjustment of the school to its environment. Anti-organisation theory, at least in some of its forms, would advocate that the mission of a Model B school should be maintained against all external pressures since this is the way to transform the education system and indeed the social system as a whole.

Conclusion

The history of organisation theory and management theory shows a move from a belief in the efficacy of Model A (bureaucracy and classical management theory) to Model B (organismic and human relations management theory). Much discussion about schools as organisations has been posed in terms of this dichotomy with a normative preference for Model B as incorporating the ideas of progressive educationists. There is a long history of attempts to establish Model B schools and in the 1960s in particular in the United States and Britain many variants of this model emerged. However, in the more radical variants – at least those about which books and articles were written – confronted a number of problems not least the problem of coping with – even in the political climate of the 1960s – a hostile environment.

Even as Model B schools were being advocated and, indeed, established, the literature contained descriptions of schools as being 'loosely structured' leading to a normative organisation theory of schools as loosely-coupled systems, a mixture of bureaucracy and human relations models with different components dealing with the routine events and the non-routine events encountered by schools, i.e. a structured quasi-bureaucratic mode for coping with the need for coordination coupled with spaces-between-structures allowing for the innovativeness and creativity which is congruent with the educational enterprise.

This approach was congruent with the emerging *contingency* theory of management which holds that different environments induce a need for different structures. Thus neither bureaucracy nor human relations models are 'better' or 'worse' than each other; either can be functional in certain contexts and some mixture of the two in other contexts. These are powerful reasons for accepting contingency loose-coupling at the theoretical level. However, there is at the moment too little empirical research to specify what patterns of mix have been effective for schools under what conditions. The problem of contingency theory is that it is difficult to specify in advance an ideal mix because environments change, even the hitherto relatively stable environment of the school, and organisations must adapt to these changes. This presents a problem for leadership which, on the one hand must create a 'mission' for the school, but on the other must have the means to modify this 'mission' in the light of changing circumstances.

Finally, one can reiterate the point that loosely-coupled and contingency theories are essentially conservative theories of adaptation rather than radical theories of change. It might be argued that the mission should be maintained at all costs in order to transform the environment itself, and if it fails it may at least have left the trace of a new order in society.

3 Organisational Pathos and the School

> The trouble with schoolmasters is that they think all problems are soluble. They aren't.
>
> STANLEY MIDDLETON *The Daysman*

There is a pathos inherent in all organisations which arises from the chronic discrepancy between proclaimed organisational goals and their achievement. The incumbent of any leadership role in any organisation is a modern Sisyphus, constantly pushing uphill a backward-rolling boulder in an effort to mobilise people and resources and move them towards an ever-receding peak. To be sure, limited objectives are constantly being achieved by the organisation as a whole or by particular groups within it. Without such achievements organisations would decay and members would remain acutely dissatisfied. But when one considers the goals which society attributes to organisations, and especially to the school, and the goals which organisations establish for themselves, the pathos is obvious.

There are a number of different reasons why this pathos is generated. One is that we tend to view organisations from a rationalistic perspective, the perspective which dominates management theory perhaps even more strongly than it dominates organisation theory. This rationalistic ideal of organisational process assumes the establishment of a clear set of achievable goals, the total commitment of organisational members to these goals, the availability of all the necessary resources, the capacity of organisational members to coordinate their activities, and the unequivocal achievement of successful outcomes. In this direction lies neuroticism, if one takes neurotics to be people who are preoccupied with the discrepancy between an ideal world which they carry around in their heads and the imperfect world of everyday experience. Of course, the great majority of organisational members do not become neurotic. For many, the organisational world of work is not a central life interest, and problems other than malfunctioning organisations engage most of their attention. And even amongst the professional and administrative classes who invest more of themselves in their work organisations, most come to terms with the shortfall between goals and their achievement. Yet there will be none for whom the organisational pathos does not lead to daily irritations.

The sources of pathos are numerous. One is the fundamental notion of organisational *goal*. It is a term much in play when professionals and administrators discuss their organisations, yet it is a term which is at best problematic and at worst valueless as a guide to organisational processes. Another is that there are inherent limits to the effective coordination of organisational activities, partly because there are too many variables entailed to achieve fully a rational coordination and partly also because there are logical limits to rationality. Thus organisational members are invariably functioning in a world of imperfect rationality. A third reason, which relates to the empirical limits to rationality, is that contemporary, industrialised and modernised societies are becoming increasingly turbulent as the result of interrelated social, political, economic and technological changes so that the best laid rational plans for an organisation are constantly buffeted and knocked off course by the squalls created by uncontrollable external circumstances.

These themes will be explored in this chapter. To focus on the limits to organisational rationality is to adopt a perspective quite different from the conventional approach which posits an ideal form of rational organisation. This focus might be dysfunctional if this were a book on the management of organisations since it is perhaps desirable that those studying management should not have their motivations impaired by considering the limits to what they can achieve. But this is a book concerned with *understanding* organisations and hence with the limitations on what can be achieved.

The problem of goals

The concept of *organisational goal* holds a powerful attraction for both administrators and theorists. One of the distinguishing characteristics of organisations as social units is that they are established for specific purposes. There can be no possible doubt that schools are established for the purpose of educating the young and school goals incorporate this purpose. The achievement of these goals is the administrator's *raison d'être*. They are the touchstone whereby the administrator can check the effectiveness of the various activities undertaken within the organisation. The headteacher proclaims the goals of the school in the school brochure, in the staff handbook and to the assembled guests on speech night. Goals give meaning to what the school *does*. Organisational theorists, or, as we have seen in Chapter 1 those of a functionalist persuasion, find the concept of goal a useful aid to the understanding of organisational processes. Goals provide a focus for their enquiries and enable them to judge the contribution of a particular activity to the whole and, if goals can be operationalised, they provide the yardstick whereby the effectiveness of an organisation can be judged both on its own terms (Is the organisation achieving the goals which it set out to achieve?) or, taking a comparative view (Of organisations A, B and C, sharing the same goals, which has been the most successful in achieving them?).

Goals may appear to offer a means of overcoming organisational pathos but in fact they actually contribute to that pathos, for the truth is that organisations need goals to give them meaning. However, when the goals *of the organisation as a whole* are subjected to close scrutiny, their value as a guide to organisational practice becomes questionable. We can examine some of the problems relating to the concept itself, the content of goals and their operationalisation.

The concept itself is extremely slippery. As Perrow (1968) puts it, 'The concept of organisational goal, like concepts of power, authority, or leadership, has been unusually resistant to precise, unambiguous definition. Yet a definition of goals is necessary and unavoidable in organisational analysis. Organisations are established to do something; they perform work directed toward some end. We must examine the end or goal if we are to analyse organisational behaviour.' This honest statement by a leading organisational analyst reveals the pathos discussed above: organisations have to have goals, we cannot quite say what they are, but we must endow them with some definition if we are to make any headway. One such definition is the following: 'By organisational goal we understand a state of the organisation as a whole toward which the organisation is moving, as evidenced by statements persons make (intentions), and activities in which they engage' (Gross, 1969). This is an adequate definition but reveals some of the difficulties inherent in the concept. One key problem is highlighted in the phrase *the organisation as a whole*. It will be clear from the discussion in Chapter 1 that a phenomenologically-inclined theorist would question whether organisations as such can be said to have goals. It would be argued that this is an unwanted reification, the attribution of a reality to an organisation which it does not have. The point would be that only *individuals* can have goals. The phenomenologist would concede that groups of individuals have common interests, and in confronting common problems can, through their interaction, come to recognise these mutual concerns and construct a set of shared goals. It is conceivable that all members of an organisation, such as a school, could thus construct a common set of shared goals, but the point would be that these would be the constructed goals of a group of people and not goals which could be objectively ascribed to the organisation as an abstract entity. In practice, it is unlikely that organisational goals would be shared to that extent. Although in the case of schools it is possible to conceive of all staff sharing the same goals, it is perhaps stretching credulity to believe that all pupils would share them as well. Thus a goals-model which assumes consensus is criticised by both phenomenologists and conflict theorists. Both argue that what are alleged to be the 'goals' of an organisation are, in fact, the goals of those who hold most power in organisations and that these are continuously contested by groups which generate alternative sets of goals. Thus, from these perspectives, organisations are areas in which sets of goals are in conflict. Another problem inherent in Gross's definition is the potential gap between the ideal and reality which is concealed by linking 'statements persons make (intentions) *and* activities'. (Italics added.) Intentions and activities will coincide only where there is either total consensus or total power to realise stated goals, a situation unlikely to occur in the real world. In the case of each of these problems we have the choice between treating a set of goals as an ideal remaining as such however far the activities of an organisation fall short of their achievement, or defining goals operationally as the commitments which different sets of participants accept.

The phenomenological and conflict critique of goals has considerable theoretical validity. However, the main significance of this critique is to alert those who run organisations, and those who study them, that a rationalistic, consensual goal-oriented model of organisations can only be an ideal. It can thus sensitise them to limitations of the idea of a shared set of goals and alert them to the validity of the goals of different individuals and groups. The critique cannot, however, dispose of the goal as a symbolic concept for the organisational leader nor as an heuristic concept guiding one approach to the study of organisations. Organisations cannot be wholly devoid of an overall purpose if they are to fulfil the expectations which they are to meet.

If one accepts the paradox that in any strict sense organisations as such cannot have goals but that they cannot function effectively without them, then one is committed to exploring the problems involved in continuing to utilise the term. The major problems are that the goals which might be hypothesised for organisations are of different kinds, are frequently expressed in abstract and non-operational terms, and they often prove to be incompatible with each other. These problems can be explored in turn.

There is a tendency for goals to be initially conceptualised in terms of organisational *output*, not necessarily a physical output as in a factory but, in education, for example, in the skills, knowledge attitudes, etc. acquired by pupils. Yet organisations can have goals other than product goals of this sort. Gross (1969) identifies five kinds of organisational goal for a university, namely:

1 *Output goals*: the inculcation of knowledge, skills and values in students.
2 *Adaptation goals*: the attraction of staff and students, the procurement of resources and the validation of the activities of the university.
3 *Management goals*: the administration of the university, the assignment of priorities, the handling of conflict.
4 *Motivation goals*: the creation of satisfaction and commitment in both staff and students.
5 *Positional goals*: the maintenance of the university's standing in relation to other universities, the improvement on this, and its defence in the face of pressures likely to reduce this standing.

This list is illustrative and is not presented as an agreed list of organisational goals. Other lists could have been suggested, e.g. Perrow (1968) which, although different in some ways, would have made the same point: that there are organisational goals *other than* the obvious output goals. It might be suggested that all the listed goals other than output goals could be reformulated as 'means'. There is some merit in this. When one considers why organisations are established in the first place – in the case of schools for the education of children – only output goals can be the 'true' goals. This broad distinction is useful in pointing to what might be an organisational pathology – a preoccupation with goals other than output goals, particularly management goals – but substantively the distinction is difficult to sustain. Just two reasons can be noted. One is that output goals by no means exhaust the purposes which organisations serve. This is particularly true of schools. It is widely considered that the *process* of schooling is as important as its product. This is held to be so because of the significance for good or ill of the 'hidden curriculum', although this raises the nice point of whether what a child acquires through the hidden curriculum should be construed as an 'output goal' or as an unanticipated consequence. But this aside, it is also held that since children spend much of their time in schools the ethos or climate of a school has an importance independent of its outputs, although one can hardly think that the two would not be related if output is interpreted broadly to cover all changes brought about in the pupil. The other point is that the balance between the various kinds of goal will shift. Although one might expect output goals to be salient, there are situations in which they may be less crucial than other goals. For example, if a school is threatened with closure due to falling rolls, the school organisation might be left to 'idle' in relation to the achievement of the output goals of pupil learning, as the goal of survival becomes salient and staff devote more of their energies toward mobilising support, attracting additional pupils to the school and furthering the school's reputation.

When school goals are articulated they tend to be simultaneously both diverse and diffuse. They are diverse because education tends to be charged with a wide range of tasks to which schools seek to respond, and diffuse because schools seek to bring about changes in pupils which are more than a particular set of knowledge, skill and attitudes. In order to illustrate this point we can consider not the goals adumbrated by a particular school but those set out in the 1977 Green Paper *Education in Schools: a Consultative Document.*

1 to help children develop lively, inquiring minds, giving them the ability to question and to argue rationally, and to apply themselves to tasks:
2 to instil respect for moral values, for other people and for oneself, and tolerance of other races, religions, and ways of life;
3 to help children understand the world in which we live, and the interdependence of nations;
4 to help children to use language effectively and imaginatively in reading, writing and speaking;
5 to help children to appreciate how the nation earns and maintains its standard of living and properly to esteem the essential role of industry and commerce in this process;
6 to provide a basis of mathematical, scientific and technical knowledge, enabling boys and girls to learn the essential skills needed in a fast changing world of work;
7 to teach children about human achievement and aspirations in the arts and sciences, in religion, and in the search for a more just social order;
8 to encourage and foster the development of the children whose social or environmental disadvantages cripple their capacity to learn, if necessary by making additional resources available to them.

We are not here concerned with whether these particular goals are appropriate to schools, but simply with taking them as examples of proclaimed goals in order to explore further the problems inherent in the concept. The first point to note is that they are both diverse and diffuse. As such they are completely open-ended. It would be impossible for schools to achieve these goals completely since they are infinite. This is made even more problematic since these goals, like the goals of most schools, are expressed in terms of the actions which the school will take and not with the outcomes of the process, the notoriously difficult-to-measure changes which have occurred in pupils as a result of their schooling. Goals can be stated in terms of expected outcomes, but this is generally resisted in education because what can be readily assessed, namely the cognitive outcomes of schooling, is regarded as representing only a limited set of school goals which would distort the purpose of the school if confined to this domain. It can be readily seen that many of the goals listed above are not measurable in this way, or achievable in any total sense. Schools must always fall short of achieving these goals and here again we see the pathos of an inevitable gap between goals and achievement. A second point is that they stand in need of far greater specification if they are to become in any sense operational. As stated, they constitute only a general set of guides to action. However, it can be argued that in an organisation such as a school which is staffed by professionals, it is sufficient for only the broadest goals to be established, thus leaving the professional with sufficient autonomy to interpret these goals in the interests of clients. A third point is that the goals may be inherently in conflict and that these conflicts will become manifest when the goals are given a specific form in terms of pedagogy and curriculum. From the list given above it could well be, for example, that in inducing children to 'esteem the essential role of industry and commerce' when expressed in a curricular form, could be in conflict with the goal of 'the search for a more just social order'. These goals are not necessarily in conflict as they stand, but they could be if each is operationalised in certain ways.

The concept of *organisational goal* is invariably problematic but is particularly so in the case of schools for the reasons stated above: that proclaimed school goals tend to be diffuse, diverse, abstract and non-operational as they stand. If one accepts that proclaimed goals perform the function of guiding the organisation, it becomes an interesting empirical problem to relate the avowed goals of a school to the activities undertaken by staff. Because of the diffuse nature of educational goals and the relative autonomy of the teacher, there is considerable opportunity for slippage between avowed goals and their implementation. A number of sources of such slippage can be noted. One is what might be called 'the strain to the instrumental'. There is a broadly accepted distinction within the social sciences between *instrumental* goals which are utilitarian and intermediate to the attainment of other goals, and *expressive* goals which are goals worthwhile in themselves. The avowed goals of many schools contain a strong expressive component, the worthwhileness in themselves of various components of the curriculum. However, because in a complex industrialised society schools perform a selecting and differentiating role in relation to the occupational structure, and since occupation is a central concern of pupils and their parents who expect schools to give some priority to this, there is a tendency for schools to give greater prominence to instrumental goals, as embodied in tests and examinations, than to expressive goals. There are few schools which give priority to expressive goals. A. S. Neill's Summerhill would be one.

Another problem is the substitution of control goals for educational goals. Control over pupils is a central organisational problem for schools. However, insofar as the control goal is stated at all, it is stated as an intermediate goal on the grounds that the end-goal of education cannot be achieved without pupil control. However, it is possible for control to become a major goal in its own right. The manner in which the substitution of goals can occur in educational organisations is neatly illustrated in *The Open Door College* by Burton Clark (1960). A junior college was established at San Jose in California with the major goal of providing a technical education for the majority of students who would enter the work force at the end of their course, and with the minor goal of providing an academic education for a small number of students who would then transfer to a university. But because of the 'open-door' policy which prevailed, students were permitted to choose their own courses, and, in fact, the majority opted for the academic (transfer) courses and only a minority opted for the technical (terminal) courses. The official goals of the school thus changed to a major commitment to an academic education and a minor commitment to a technical education. But since, in the view of the teachers, many of the students enrolling for the academic course did not have the necessary aptitudes, the goal of 'cooling out' the students perceived as academically incompetent was substituted for the goal of teaching these students. A variety of techniques was evolved for persuading such students to drop academic courses in favour of technical courses. For example, counsellors used various kinds of data about students to convince them to withdraw from the transfer courses. 'Need for Improvement' notices were used (as Burton Clark put it: 'If the student did not seek advice, advice sought him'). A course entitled Psychology 5: Orientation to College, compulsory for all transfer students, was designed to encourage the students to make a careful appreciation of their capacity to achieve college entrance by inviting them to compare their own grade point averages and scores on various aptitude tests with those required by colleges.

It is clear from the above discussion of organisational goals in general and school goals in particular that the concept generates considerable theoretical and practical problems. Organisational pathos is inherent in schools since proclaimed goals are frequently unattainable, and thus all schools are thereby 'underachieving'. There is a proclivity for proclaimed goals to be substituted by others through the everyday practices of teachers. Insofar as there is a consciousness of this, it yields further scope for pathos. Moreover, as Musgrove (1971) has pointed out, schools are underpowered for the goals they are expected to achieve.

There is clearly much to be said for the phenomenological critique of the concept of organisational goals. Goals are declaimed by organisational élites who make efforts to have them accepted as operational guides to organisational activities. But since individual members of one organisation may have their own contrary goals, and since there is great opportunity for slippage between proclaimed goals and operating norms, it is better to focus on the organisation as an area of conflicting perspectives on what *ought* to be done, and to note only that certain 'goals' of certain individuals and groups emerge as dominant. Thus the problem of goals is transformed into a problem of power. And yet it is not wholly possible to dispose of goals in this way. Where the outcome of internal competition results in an organisation pursuing 'goals' which are strongly at odds with the mandate bestowed by society, then sanctions might well be imposed. High level abstract goals at least give some indication of a general expectation of what a school ought to be doing, and as such they at least give some broad direction to the organisation.

The limits to rationality

Organisational pathos is endemic because organisations are chronically incapable of achieving the goals which stakeholders and their own members set for them and because, except in relation to limited objectives or through the subjective sense of achievement of members, they are incapable of demonstrating their success in achieving these goals. An associated source of organisational pathos arises from the fact that there is a chronic discrepancy between the 'rational' model of organisation, which holds considerable appeal for those who manage, and the less-than-rational reality of life in organisations. Three limitations of rationality can be considered: the *phenomenological* critique of rationality as a universal concept, the critique of those who note the *cognitive* limits to rationality, i.e. the limitations imposed by the limits to human capacities for ordering and relating data – advances in computing notwithstanding – and the *logical* limits to rationality wherein a 'rational' organisation is inherently unattainable.

It is impossible in a relatively short section to mount a full discussion of the concept of rationality in its full philosophical splendour. It is perhaps sufficient to note here that the scientific means-ends rationality which underpins much organisation theory, and particularly management theory, is widely contested. It is argued that this is not the only form which rationality can take. It is also argued that a distinction can be made between the form of rationality which may be appropriate for certain purposes, particularly scientific research and a different everyday or common sense rationality which enables people to cope quite adequately with their lives. It is further argued that rationality is not universal and independent of interests but in fact flows from those interests. There are some enormously complicated issues here which have been much debated by philosophers and social scientists. One might dispute, for example, the rationality of the rain dance of the Hopi Indians and the witchcraft of the Azande tribe. These are not 'rational' activities according to the Western scientific notion of rationality because there can be no scientific cause and effect relationship between witchcraft and the cure of disease, or between a tribal dance and the appearance of rain, but they may well be 'rational' when perceived from within the culture of the tribe since these activities have functions other than their manifest functions. From the perspective of management, the action of workers in taking strike action may well be irrational since the result could involve a loss of income by the workers. However, leaving aside the question of whether such a loss actually ensued, the strike might well have been 'rational' in terms of the workers' perceptions of their longer term interests or in terms of their need to demonstrate solidarity. Likewise pupils behave highly 'irrationally' when their behaviour is viewed from the teachers' perspective in which rationality might be seen as the maximisation of individual academic attainment. Pupils have other interests – the pleasures of 'messing about', prestige in the peer group, outside jobs, etc. – and their school behaviour may well be 'rational' in terms of these interests. Thus, leaving aside whether or not there is a single form of rationality founded on the principles of the natural sciences, there will be in all organisations competing 'rationalities' arising from differences of real interests or perceived interests which will lead to a gap between the goals of management and their achievement.

Even if one accepts the possibility of a rational model of organisation, there are cognitive limits to rationality. This has been the main theme of the influential writings on organisation by Simon (1964) and March and Simon (1958). Simon recognised that the model of 'economic man' who could be expected to optimise his interests by making rational choices was an inadequate account of organisational behaviour. He therefore substituted the concept of 'administrative man' whose rationality is bounded or limited and who, since he cannot know all the choice alternatives when making a decision 'satisfices' rather than maximises. March and Simon write:

> Most human decision-making, whether individual, or organisational, is concerned with the discovery or selection of satisfactory alternatives, only in exceptional cases is it concerned with the selection of optional alternatives.

March and Simon compare the two processes of *optimising* and *satisficing* with looking for the sharpest needle in the haystack and looking for a needle which is sharp enough to sew with. The assumptions of the classical model are that all choice alternatives are known, that all the consequences of choosing each alternative are known, and that individuals can order these consequences in terms of utility. It is clear that all this is a well-nigh unattainable set of criteria and hence the actor is forced to 'satisfice'. This occurs according to the actor's necessarily limited definition of the situation which is only an approximate model of the 'real' situation. However, March and Simon do not deny rationality in organisational choice, they believe that the actor can achieve a *bounded rationality*. They hold that members work with simplified models which involve, for example, attending to a restricted range of situations and the pursuit of semi-independent or loosely-coupled actions. At the policy level, 'political' challenges to over-rationalistic 'economic' approaches was mounted in the 1950s and subsequently by Lindblom, in his notion of 'the science of muddling through', and others (cf. Dahl and Lindblom, 1953; Braybrooke and Lindblom, 1963; Lindblom 1959, 1966, 1968). The empirical problem of rationality in organisations is exacerbated by the increasing turbulence of organisational environments. Organisations have long been recognised as being *open-systems* which entails their internal activities being open to influence to a greater or lesser degree by external circumstance. It is difficult to demonstrate that organisations are now, to a greater degree than in the past, subjected to more internal pressures from outside sources, but it would seem to be the case. Schon (1971) for example, argues that we have gone 'beyond the stable state'. He writes: 'Throughout our society we are experiencing the actual or theoretical dissolution of stable organisations and institutions, actions for personal identity and systems of values.' It does appear as though the rate of change, perhaps stemming mainly from technological development and the growing interdependence of social institutions, is accelerating and thus generating an increasingly turbulent environment in which organisations must function. This trend can be seen in relation to the schools. Once considered a 'domesticated' organisation which could continue placidly to pursue its goals without need to compete in the marketplace like the 'wild' organisations of the business world (Carlson, 1964), the declining birthrate with consequently falling enrolments has put the continued existence of many schools in doubt. Moreover, schools have become more interdependent with other forms of organisation and social institution – commercial, industrial, welfare, legal, community, political, etc. – and the once-strong boundary around the school has become more permeable. The school has become a more open system and has to take into account more, and frequently competing, factors in its decision-making. Thus the cognitive limits to rationality become more acute as the school seeks to take into account the expectations of various sets of stakeholders who are increasingly taking to forms of pressure group activity.

Finally, there is the question of the logical as well as cognitive limits to rationality. There is actually little work on the limits to rationality in schools, or indeed on organisations generally. The writers who have made the greatest contributions to this issue have been more concerned with the limits as they operate in the area of public policy (e.g. Olson, 1965; Hirschman, 1978, 1981). The most wide-ranging and fruitful discussion occurs in a series of books by Elster (1978, 1979). It is not possible to explore these ideas in detail, but essentially they are concerned with the ways in which the rational pursuit of ends by any single individual has an unanticipated outcome of preventing the achievement of those ends when all individuals in the relevant set pursue the same end in a rational manner. For example, in the present context of high youth unemployment it is rational for the individuals to seek to improve their employability by enhancing their educational qualifications. However, if all school leavers maximised their qualifications and no additional jobs were available, employers would increase their demand for qualifications and thus school leavers would be no better off. The individual can only succeed by increasing qualifications whilst others fail to do so.

A similar problem is that of promotion in a context of declining opportunities. Given the present salary structure and status differences, the teacher is in the same position as the school leaver described above. Promotion will go to those who acquire the qualifications, using this term broadly to include not only academic qualifications but in-service training and experience of various kinds. But if all teachers pursue the 'rational' courses of obtaining qualifications, none will be better off.

Another fruitful area of analysis would be participation in decision-making. Without entering into a long discussion on the various connotations of *democracy*, it can be seen that insofar as individuals increase control over their own actions, the ultimate outcome may be a reduction of the capacity of all members to attain their individual ends. This can be seen to be the case in those schools which have been able to adapt thoroughgoing patterns of internal democracy. There has been a tendency for those schools to fall short of fulfilling the aspirations of members. It may be that this has been due to an inability to establish appropriate patterns of decision-making, or to respond to the pressures of a hostile environment, but the discrepancy between aspiration and achievement is logically inherent in the attempt to maximise organisational democracy. Elster (1978) quotes Simmel (1968) as stating: 'The all-and-out democrat will not be governed, even if this means that he cannot be served either.' Although Simmel made this statement in relation to the American political system, it can equally well apply to some attempts to democratise school. In Swidler's study (1979) of two highly democratised high schools in California, the power of the students was such that it negated the efforts of school leaders to meet the aspirations of the very same students.

On garbage cans and organised anarchies

Because of the diversity and diffuseness of educational goals and the inevitable limits to rationality in all organisations, the conversion of goals into issues for discussion and decision-making becomes a highly problematic affair. The day-to-day problem of teaching provides the school with a basic stability and predictability, although this is not to say that teaching is an essentially routine process. But at the level of policy, issues emerge and disappear again in ways which are far from predictable. The source of an issue, how it becomes an agenda item, the range of people engaged in the issue, the intensity of the involvement, the direction of that intensity, and the fate of the issue – whether it leads to a decision, to the implementation of the decision, or to the demise of the issue without discernible effect upon the school – are matters which have only been considered rarely in the application of organisational theory to schools, and even less frequently have they been the subject for research. The prevailing model is still underpinned by rationalistic assumptions of goal-setting, decision-making and implementation. However, one theorist who has been attentive to the idiosyncratic nature of organisational decision-making is James March whose work we can briefly consider as providing an appropriate backdrop to the discussion in the remainder of this chapter.

The collection of papers edited by March and Olsen (1976) questions the fit between the organisational theory and the real world of organisations. In particular, March and his colleagues question the received wisdom about how decisions are made and implemented. They note that this process hardly conforms to the rationalistic paradigm of management theory. The history of the decision-making process in organisations is extremely haphazard, with decisions keenly contested at some times but not at others, with disputes over participating rights sometimes more significant than the issues themselves, with decisions sometimes taken after lengthy and serious discussion, but at other times decisions taken matter-of-factly by a limited number of people. They note that the process of making an organisational choice is often an opportunity for much else, for fulfilling duties, for defining virtue, for distributing praise and blame, for discovering and expressing self interests, and for the sheer pleasure of being involved in the occasion of making a choice as a decision.

This complexity is increased by the high degree of ambiguity which prevails in organisations, and it can be noted that the diverse goals of schools make them particularly prone to ambiguity. March and his colleagues identify four particular types of opaqueness or ambiguity in organisations: *intention* (i.e. existence of ill-defined and inconsistent objectives), *understanding* (i.e. the difficulty involved in interpreting the organisational world, its technology and environmental pressures), *history* (i.e. the difficulty in interpreting the organisation's history and its present consequences) and *organisation* (i.e. the variations in the time and attention which individuals give to decisions from one choice occasion to another). The problematic nature of organisational goals and individual preferences, the lack of clarity about how the organisation 'works' and the fluidity of participation lead them to part the now-famous *garbage-can model of organisational choice*. Rather than decision-making following the apparently rational process of weighing alternatives between organisational goals and then between the different means of achieving these goals, a decision comes out of the 'garbage can' into which have gone four 'streams'. These are as follows:

1. *Problems* Problems are the concern of people inside and outside the organisation. They arise over issues of lifestyle: family; frustrations of work; careers; group relations within the organisation; distribution of status, jobs, and money; ideology; or current crises of mankind as interpreted by the mass media or the nextdoor neighbour. All require attention. Problems are, however, distinct from choices, and they may not be resolved when choices are made.

2. *Solutions* A solution is somebody's product. A computer is not just a solution to a problem in payroll management,

discovered when needed. It is an answer actively looking for a question. The creation of need is not solely a curiosity of the market in consumer products; it is a general phenomenon of processes of choice. Despite the dictum that you cannot find the answer until you have formulated the question, you often do not know the question in organisational problem solving until you know the answer.

3 *Participants* Participants come and go. Since every entrance is an exit somewhere else, the distribution of 'entrances' depends on the attributes of the choice being left as much as it does on the attributes of the new choice. Substantial variation in participation stems from other demands on the participants' time (rather than from features of the decision under study).

4 *Choice opportunities* These are occasions when an organisation is expected to produce behaviour that can be called a decision. Opportunities arise regularly and any organisation has ways of declaring an occasion for choice. Contracts must be signed; people hired, promoted, or fired; money spent; and responsibilities allocated.

They summarise the process as follows:

> The garbage can process, as it has been observed, is one in which problems, solutions and participants move from one choice opportunity to another in such a way that the nature of the choice, the time it takes, and the problems it solves all depend on a relatively complicated intermeshing of the mix of choices available at any one time, the mix of problems that have access to the organisation, the mix of solutions looking for problems, and the outside demands on the decision makers.

The concept of the garbage can is linked to another concept which has become popular in the recent literature on organisations, presumably because it resonates with the experience of theorists and participants (and theorists-as-participants, for it must be remembered that organisation theorists usually work in organisations). This is the concept of *organised anarchy*. Weiner, in March and Olsen op cit., writes:

> In these conceptions an organised anarchy is an organisation typified by unclear goals, poorly understood technology, and variable participation.

The above summary of some of the elements in March's approach to organisation is necessarily concentrated and the reader should read March and Olsen's collection for an elaboration and for an account of case studies which explore organisational decision-making with the aid of these concepts, case studies which deal mainly with educational settings of different kinds. Some critics of March claim that he has overemphasised the degree of ambiguity and anarchy in organisations. Against this, it must be said that March does not wholly throw out the baby with the bath water. He believes that rationality is present in organisational decision-making but simply notes that organisational choices get made sometimes in rather odd ways and always in conditions much more complex and adventitious than conventional theory allows. As such, it is an attractive and prima facie compelling view of organisations. Against this necessarily condensed theoretical background we can now consider some aspects of school decision-making.

The succession of goals

This phenomenon has long had a place in the literature on organisations. However, it has usually been applied to organisations which survive by moving successively from one goal to another as each is fulfilled, or as particular goals become less significant for the supporting environment. The classic case in the literature is the American Infantile Paralysis Association which, as the cause for which it was founded ceased to be important when the incidence of infantile paralysis dramatically decreased, moved on to other charitable concerns (Sills, 1957). However, the 'succession of goals' concept has not been generally applied to 'domesticated' organisations, nor has it been informed by the insights of March and colleagues into organisational choice.

A school can be said to be characterised by a 'succession of goals'. As was noted in the previous section, schools have a very broad set of agreed goals which, whilst they are expressed at the most general level, are uncontroversial and schools can always claim to be pursuing these generalised goals as, indeed, they are. The issue of the succession of goals comes at the point where schools convert these goals into *commitments* (Corwin, 1965), and make choices between the alternatives which are competing for attention at any given time. March's approach takes over when it becomes a question of determining by what process particular goals become salient and what factors lead to choices being made. There are enormous conceptual difficulties in such an enterprise, not least in defining what is an *issue*. The possible elements in what might be said to constitute an issue are its significance for the effectiveness of the school, the intensity of feelings amongst the staff, the number and hierarchical status of staff engaged in the making of choices, and the expectations of outsiders. Each of these is capable of independent variation. Thus one need not elaborate the difficulties entailed in understanding the ebb and flow of issues. There are very few studies of what can be termed 'the natural history of issues' from which generalisations, if such there are, can be drawn. The methodological problems involved in such a study need not be elaborated. Unless a researcher was immersed in a school over a long period of time and able to detect the first showings of what was to become an issue, studies would need to become *post hoc* with all the attendant problems of recall and re-interpretation by participants.

There are thus very few cases studies of the natural history of an issue in schools, but one exception is Christensen's (1976) study of a Danish free school in which three apparently unequivocal decisions were made: to establish a 'Society of Friends of the School', to change the school to a non-graded pattern of organisation for instruction, and to rehire a teacher who had been dismissed. Yet none of these decisions was implemented. In order to explain this rather surprising fact he calls upon the 'garbage can' model and makes the following points: that the *outcome* of a decision is often less important than the *process*, that implementation is in the hands of people who have the resources but who might not share the attitudes of the decision-making group. ('Votes count but resources decide': Rokkan, 1968.) The high level of attention to the making of a decision may not be sustained through to its implementation, and, finally, the fact that other problems come to absorb the allocation of the organisation as new crises arise.

The unpredictable character of the natural history of issues in schools arises because they have the following characteristics:

1 The diffuseness and diversity of goals means that only a very limited number can have the attention of the school at any time.

2 The diversity of goals means that issues will arise from a variety of sources, e.g. LEA requirements, the imperatives of a national report or the report of an HMI visit, parental pressures, adventitious issues arising accidentally (perhaps literally arising from an accident), the head's identification of important issues, the emergence of an issue from a staff analysis of problems and needs, the persistence of an individual member of staff in pursuit of an interest which may sometimes take on the character of an *idée fixe*.

3 The ambiguous nature of the decision-making system of the school in which the head has a high degree of authority but generally establishes some pattern for involving colleagues. Since teacher involvement in consultation is voluntary, participation will be variable. There might be a high initial involvement which drops away as the daily imperatives of teaching reassert themselves, and as teachers 'discover' that their personal interests are not involved. On the other hand, there might be a limited initial involvement which grows as teachers recognise the significance of the issue. Or this might be an in-and-out involvement with a consequent loss of continuity and the introduction of new opinions, or the affirmation of new interests over time.

4 There is, as Christensen noted, often a division between those who decide upon a choice and those with executive power. It is usually the head who has the executive power and there may be a disjunction between decision and implementation (see Bailey, 1982a).

5 The loosely-coupled nature of the school means that although the head, as chief executive, can implement some decisions which have obvious school-wide and structural consequences, there are other decisions, usually affecting classroom practice, which are less easily implemented. A choice is made, but nothing happens. This is a situation of 'innovation without change'. There is a symbolic acceptance of a decision but practice remains the same.

Conclusion

One volume of Isiah Berlin's collected writings is entitled *Against the Current*. The 'current' is the developing belief in the rationality, or the promise of rationality, in human affairs with the growing application to these affairs of the procedures of the natural sciences. The papers in that volume celebrate those writers who have perceived the inherent limits to scientific rationality and have stressed the idiosyncratic, adventitious, unpredictable and intractable nature of human action. The rationalistic 'current' has dominated management theory and, with some exceptions and until recently, organisation theory. Yet anyone who observes organisations closely, or who tries to run an organisation, is aware of their less-than-rational, even chaotic, nature and the unpredictable pebbles which derail the best-laid plans. The less-than-rational nature of policy-making and implementation even at the highest levels has been revealed in Allison's (1971) study of the Cuban missile crisis and the comments by Zbigniew Brzezinski, President Carter's adviser on national security, that history is the reflection of continuing chaos rather than consciously formulated policies (Urban, 1981). Of the less lethal level of the educational system Kogan (1975) has written that it is 'pluralistic, incremental and reactive'. And life in schools is certainly no more rational than in the educational system as a whole.

This chapter has explored the aleatory aspects of the school as an organisation by pursuing two themes. One was the slippery concept of *organisational goal*. Although most schools will certainly move in some broad direction, the notion of a set of goals to which all the components are geared fails to correspond to the reality which is that insofar as a school has specific goals these will emerge from the interplay of interests within the school. A second was the inescapable limits to the particular kind of means-ends rationality which pervades the natural sciences in the contexts of social affairs. The limits arise from the fact that there are competing rationalities which are the outcome of different interests, the cognitive limits to rationality which arise because not all possibilities can be conceived in the planning process, and logical limits to rationality which arise because individual rationality can engender collective irrationality. These limitations were illuminated by reference to the work of March and others who have written 'against the current' in organisation theory.

This rationality-questioning perspective raises a problem for those who run organisations and the management theory which is designed to guide their efforts. To *understand* organisations may be to detract from the task of *running* them. However, as noted, the work of Simon, March and Lindblom does not characterise organisations as wholly, or even mainly, irrational. They are probably more rational than they are adventitious and the quest for rational procedures is not misplaced. However, organisational pathos will remain and rationalistic approaches will always be blown off course by the contingent, the unexpected and the irrational.

4 Powerful Heads and Professional Teachers

> Headmasters have power at their disposal with which Prime Ministers have never yet been invested.
>
> WINSTON CHURCHILL *My Early Life*

It is ritualistic for anyone writing about *power, influence* and *authority* to state that these constitute three of the most slippery concepts in the social sciences. Hundreds of books and articles by psychologists, sociologists, anthropologists and political theorists have been devoted to their definition and, less frequently, to their measurement. There is reasonable consensus on a basic definition of *power*. Many writers accept Weber's formulation: 'Power is the probability that one actor within a social relationship will be in a position to carry out his own will, despite resistance, and regardless of the basis on which this probability rests' (Weber, 1947), but difficulties arise when one comes to amplify this definition. There is far less consensus about definitions of *authority* and *influence* and, indeed, these concepts, together with *power*, have sometimes been treated as synonyms. In the absence of consensus, and in order to avoid adding further to the present confusion by adumbrating additional definitions, those given by Bacharach and Lawler (1980) will be adopted, partly because they are a relatively recent set of definitions and are therefore based on much previous work, partly because they are specifically concerned with power, influence and authority in organisations, but largely because their distinctions are the closest to the present writer's preferred usage. These definitions will be considered in abstract terms in the next section, and in subsequent sections consideration will be given to their general applicability to the school, the special problem of power and authority in organisations staffed by professionals, and the related problem of teacher participation in the decision-making process of the school.

Concepts of power, influence and authority

Bacharach and Lawler consider *power* to be a sensitising concept, that is a concept which, though lacking precision, directs us towards certain important issues. The concept of *power* gains precision only as its inherent complexities are unpacked and given a specific form. Bacharach and Lawler begin this process by distinguishing between the *form* and the *content* of power. It is unnecessary for the present argument to consider the three *forms* of *relational, dependency* and *sanction* – which they discuss in detail – but it would be useful at this point to elaborate three aspects of the *content* of power, namely *sources, types* and *bases*.

They distinguish between four *sources* of power.

Structural: power as a property of a person's office or structural position.
Personality: power as a function of personal characteristics, such as charisma or leadership qualities.
Expertise: power as a function of specialised knowledge or skill or access to information.
Opportunity: power as a function of the occupancy of roles which even though they may rank low in the hierarchy, provide the opportunity to exert power through the control of information, or key organisational tasks.

They distinguish between two *types* of power: *authority* and *influence*. As noted above, these two concepts, plus the concept of power, have been related to each other in a variety of ways in the literature and sometimes used synonymously. However, Bacharach and Lawler's distinction, though they are by no means the first writers to distinguish the three concepts in this way, is a valuable one. *Power* is the basic, generic term underpinning the other two. *Authority* is that form of power which stems from the legal right to make decisions governing others. *Influence* is that form of power which stems from the capacity to shape decisions by informal or non-authoritative means. Bacharach and Lawler make a number of further distinctions between authority and influence which it is worthwhile repeating in full.

1 Authority is the static, structural aspect of power in organisations; influence is the dynamic, tactical element.

2 Authority is the formal aspect of power; influence is the informal aspect.
3 Authority refers to the formally sanctioned right to make final decisions; influence is not sanctioned by the organisation and is, therefore, not a matter of organisational rights.
4 Authority implies involuntary submission by subordinates; influence implies voluntary submission and does not necessarily entail a superior-subordinate relationship.
5 Authority flows downward, and it is unidirectional; influence is multidirectional and can flow upward, downward or horizontally.
6 The source of authority is solely structural; the source of influence may be personal characteristics expertise, or opportunity.
7 Authority is circumscribed, that is, the domain, scope, and legitimacy of the power are specifically and clearly delimited; influence is uncircumscribed, that is, its domain, scope, and legitimacy are typically ambiguous.

Finally, Bacharach and Lawler identify four *bases* of power. Here they draw upon Etzioni (1975) who identified three bases of power: *coercive*, the ability to apply the threat of physical sanctions; *remunerative*, the control of material resources and favours; and *normative*, the control of symbolic rewards. Bacharach and Lawler have added a fourth to these which is *knowledge*, i.e. access to information as a basis of power.

It is clear that the sources, bases and types of power can be related to each other in a variety of ways giving different configurations. There is little point in exploring the possible combinations in the abstract, rather we can turn straight to the school and explore the dominant configuration with its possible variants.

Authority and influence in the school

The distinctive configuration of power relationships in the school is shaped by the interpenetration of the authority and influence of the head and the influence of teachers. The head enjoys a high degree of authority but there are constraints on its exercise which leads to a greater reliance on a wide range of both sources and bases of influence. These restraints on the head's authority include: the loosely-coupled structure of the school, expectations about the appropriateness of the exercise of authority in culturally and morally oriented organisations, and the countervailing resources of influence enjoyed by a professional staff.

We can consider the power resources of the head by utilising Bacharach and Lawler's classifications. The head has a high degree of legal authority. This is mediated through the LEA and boards of governors and managers, but *de facto* the head is responsible for the internal activities of the school and has power to control these activities. Thus the head has a clear *structural* source of authority and the ultimate base of this authority is *coercion*. In terms of the authority relationship, teachers are expected to carry out the instructions of the head. Of course, teachers have access to forms of countervailing influence to protect themselves from the potentially-coercive basis of the head's authority, but ultimately heads have legal sanctions which enable them to ensure that what they will to happen, happens. This legal sanction is the authority to initiate procedures for dismissal. Heads cannot, of course, dismiss a teacher and their power in this respect is limited by that of the governors and the LEA, but authority to initiate proceedings remains a powerful resource. In practice, this authority normally remains latent. Cases where the head has need to resort to legal sanctions are very rare. The head will reach back up the hierarchy of authority only as a last resort, partly because it is a serious step to take and partly because there is an expectation that influence should suffice in a professionally-staffed organisation, and to invoke authority, except in the most extreme cases of staff indiscipline, is to suggest a lack of leadership skills. The existence of this authority in a latent form presents a number of theoretical and empirical problems. One could never tell when a head was controlling the behaviour of others through latent legal authority or through influence. Probably not even an investigation into the perceptions of heads and teachers would enable us to disentangle latent authority and influence. The difficulty is compounded in two ways. One is that there is amongst teachers an automatic deference towards the office of headteacher, which leads to an unreflecting acceptance of the orders, suggestions and requests of heads. The Bacharach and Lawler classification would not appear to deal with this issue and it is perhaps best treated as a fifth basis of power. The head's 'suggestions' are for the most part accepted without reflection simply because they stem from the office of head. The teacher does not reflect on the legal basis of the requests. This is perhaps more akin to Weber's concept of 'traditional' authority rather than his concept of 'legal' authority. The second compounding problem is that the head's influence has a number of sources and a number of bases, so that it would be extremely rare to be able to attribute a teacher's response to a request, suggestion or order to any single source.

The personality of the head is a source of influence. Some heads have considerable charisma which would lead to their requests being fulfilled even if they did not hold an office carrying authority. They also have expertise which takes at least two forms. One is what might be called 'educational' expertise which would be an amalgam of former teaching experience, subject matter knowledge, and a knowledge of curriculum and policy issues. The other is what can be called 'administrative' expertise, the ability to run the school effectively. The head has access to the third source: opportunity. Bacharach and Lawler appear almost to confine this to the lower participants in an organisation, people who, though they have little authority, can nevertheless have a considerable influence on the school because of their access to information, resources or key tasks. The influence of secretaries and caretakers is often discussed in staffrooms although evidence for this influence is in short supply. However, there is no reason to confine opportunity to lower participants and, if applied to the head, it is clear that his opportunities for influence considerably exceed those of any other member of the school staff.

Heads have access to each of the four bases of power identified by Bacharach and Lawler. Coercion has already been discussed. They have remunerative authority and influence through their freedom to allocate resources, recommend promotions and write references for teachers who are candidates for other posts. They can exercise normative control through a variety of means: an emphasis on professional or moral values, the bestowal of praise and blame, and the symbolic significance of the allocation of such resources as rooms, classes, invitations to represent the school, etc. And they can exert influence via their control over information especially as the head is the one member of staff with a knowledge of the school as a whole and the person who has the widest and most extensive connections with outside bodies—the governors, the LEA, the Parent-Teacher Association, the social services, in-service training agencies—which provide them with rich sources of information.

With this repertoire of resources, it is hardly surprising that people judge the headteacher to have a high degree of power. However, teachers themselves are not without considerable resources of power. The question of whether teachers have any authority vis-à-vis school policy is a difficult one to answer for two reasons. One is the difficulty of determining whether any authority which they exercise is autonomous or delegated. The other turns on the issue of whether there are two forms of power—bureaucratic and professional—with teachers having access only to the second. This is a question to which we will return in the next section. We will consider here only the question of delegated authority. Bacharach and Lawler argue that authority is a dichotomous variable: someone either has power or has not. It makes little sense to speak of a person having *some* authority, although it is quite possible to speak of a person as having *some* influence. If this is so, it raises conceptual and empirical questions which have not been confronted in relation to schools. Schools have hierarchies, much more elaborate in extent in secondary than in primary schools. At each level of the hierarchy, teachers are undertaking tasks in a context of ostensible authority. The question is whether, in fact, they have the authority to undertake these tasks or whether it is only delegated with only the head having genuine authority, although even this is constrained by external control. Do teachers have the authority to teach in whichever way they wish? Do heads have the authority to require teachers to teach in a certain way? In Bacharach and Lawler's argument, teachers cannot have *some* authority and therefore must have complete authority or delegated authority. Likewise, do heads of department have complete or delegated authority over the curriculum area which they oversee? As teachers do not have full authority, presumably it is delegated from the heads and, if necessary heads can intervene and insist on a particular curriculum or style of pedagogy. This would appear to be the case. However, it would seem to be relatively rare for this to become an area of direct conflict. This is ensured by heads' latent authority, teachers' acceptance of this, heads' ample resources of influence, and the teachers' countervailing resources of influence.

Teachers have structurally-related authority over children and – if located in the higher reaches of the hierarchy – over colleagues. However, as noted above, it is difficult to be certain whether or not this authority is wholly delegated or whether there is an alternative professional basis of authority. Teachers have access to influence deriving from personality, expertise and opportunity. The place of expertise in the influence system of the school presents an interesting problem, a problem common to all organisations which employ professionals. The role of the head is conceptualised as combining professional leadership with administrative responsibilities. However, the head cannot embody all the professional expertise which a school needs. Hence teachers with specific kinds of expertise in various aspects of curriculum and pedagogy will be in a position to exercise considerable influence on the decision-making process in the school. Teachers are also in a position to exercise considerable influence through their opportunities to control information, resources, etc.

Thus the school is a complex configuration of authority and influence. The specific configuration of a particular school will turn on the formal procedures which are established for the interplay of authority and influence in the decision-making process, which will themselves be shaped by the administrative style of the head, and upon the less formal micropolitical use of influence which will be considered in a later chapter. In considering the former we will discuss first the inherent conflict between bureaucracy and professionality and then the decision-making structures appropriate to professionally-staffed organisations.

Professionally-staffed organisations

There exists a substantial literature concerned with the conflicts inherent in organisations which are staffed by professionals. It is held that the two forms of authority – bureaucratic and professional – are endemically opposed. Corwin (1965) writes: 'The school is simultaneously organised around contradictory bureaucratic and professional principles'. In Chapter 2 we briefly considered the nature of bureaucracy. We can now consider the nature of professionality.

We can begin with the functionalist notion of the nature of a profession, that is, the conception of professions as relatively distinct kinds of occupation which fulfil a crucial social function which results in those occupations having certain rights and responsibilities. Elsewhere the present writer has summarised this perspective as follows (Hoyle, 1980):

1. A profession is an occupation which performs a crucial social function.
2. The exercise of this function requires a considerable degree of skill.
3. This skill is exercised in situations which are not wholly routine but in which new problems and situations have to be handled.
4. Thus, although knowledge gained through experience is important, this recipe-type knowledge is insufficient to meet professional demands and the practitioner has to draw on a body of systematic knowledge.
5. The acquisition of this body of knowledge and the development of specific skills requires a lengthy period of higher education.
6. This period of education and training also involves the process of socialisation into professional values.
7. These values tend to centre on the pre-eminence of clients' interests and to some degree they are made explicit in a code of ethics.
8. Because knowledge-based skills are exercised in non-routine situations, it is essential for the professional to have the freedom to make his own judgements with regard to appropriate practice.
9. Because professional practice is so specialised, the organised profession should have a strong voice in the shaping of relevant public policy, a large degree of control over the exercise of professional responsibilities, and a high degree of autonomy in relation to the state.
10. Lengthy training, responsibility and client centredness are necessarily rewarded by high prestige and a high level of remuneration.

Perhaps two themes are salient on this notion of a profession: knowledge and autonomy, and it is these two characteristics which are undermined in bureaucratic organisations. Professional practice is predicated on the notion of qualified persons having the freedom to exercise their knowledge and skill in the interests of their clients in situations where routine solutions are inapplicable. In limiting the scope of the practitioner's autonomy through rules, procedures and close hierarchical control, bureaucracy is inimical to this view of professional tasks.

The bureaucratic-professional conflict is a useful heuristic starting point for a discussion of power and influence in schools. It touches on a substantive issue which can perhaps be conveyed by the following hypothetical exchange (Hoyle, 1981)

Head: 'I'm a little concerned Mr Dingle, that your English lessons pay little attention to inculcating good standards in written English.'

Dingle: 'I'm sorry to hear that, but I would like to know how you have come to your views on what goes on in my classes, and as a Physicist, what knowledge you have in the teaching of English?'

Head: 'Mr Dingle, I regard those two questions as impertinent. I know what goes on in your classroom because I hear from other members of staff and from disgruntled parents who have been to complain. And although I am a Physicist, I have been in this game long enough to know something about the teaching of English. In any case, as head of this school I am responsible for what goes on in it, and I don't like what I hear of your approach to the subject'.

Dingle: 'I'm sorry to hear that, headmaster, but as a professional I must insist on teaching English in the best way I know how.'

This vignette raises a number of issues about the validity of information available to heads, administrative style and professional behaviour, but at the centre of the exchange is the issue of whose authority counts, or should count.

Corwin (1965) made the following distinctions (see Table 5) between the expectations entailed in the two forms of organisation. Corwin is correct in seeing these in essence as contradictory principles, but at an empirical level the important questions are how they interpenetrate in practice and, at a theoretical level, how they might do so. However, one problem with Corwin's dichotomy is that the professional model, like many conceptualisations of professionality, is implicitly based on the notion of the independent professional such as a general medical practitioner who has an autonomous professional

Table 5

Organisational characteristics	Bureaucratic-employee expectations	Professional-employee expectations
Standardisation: Routine of work Continuity of procedure Specificity of rules	Stress on uniformity of clients' problems Stress on records and files Rules stated as universals, and specific	Stress on uniqueness of clients' problems Stress on research and change Rules states as alternatives, and diffuse
Specialization: Basis of division of labour	Stress on efficiency of techniques: task orientation	Stress on achievement of goals: client orientation
Basis of skill	Skill based primarily on practice	Skill based primarily on monopoly of knowledge
Authority: Responsibility for decision-making	Decisions concerning application of rules to routine problems	Decisions concerning policy in professional matters and unique problems
Basis of authority	Rules sanctioned by the public	Rules sanctioned by legally sanctioned professions
	Loyalty to the organisation and to superiors Authority from office (position)	Loyalty to professional associations and clients Authority from personal competence)

authority which is not available to professionals in organisations since some degree of coordination (or integration in the case of collegial authority to be discussed below) is essential. Thus the question becomes one of the patterns of interaction, of rider and horse rather than of two war horses pawing the ground in a head to head conflict. We are, of course, back to the concept of loosely-coupled organisation whereby structural looseness is mirrored by a similar looseness in patterns of control and autonomy. We can explore some of these interactions.

The first point to be made in the light of the discussion of power, influence and authority above, is that it is misleading to talk about a conflict between bureaucratic authority and professional authority in schools, although it might be a relevant distinction to make in the case of, for example, hospitals. The fact of the matter is that heads have a power based on legal authority whereas teachers have influence based on professional expertise. At the end of the line, authority prevails over influence. Unless Mr Dingle could influence the head by the soundness of his professional arguments, and in the vignette he makes no attempt to do so, the head's authority will prevail. The teacher's 'protection' against the authority of the head stems from the loosely-coupled character of the school and the relative insulation of the teacher when engaged in the core task of teaching.

A second problem with the simple bureaucratic-professional dichotomy is that in the case of the school we cannot label the head as a bureaucrat and the teacher as a professional. The head, too, is a professional. Nor can one avoid the problem by labelling the head as an 'administrative professional' as an alternative formulation to the head-as-bureaucrat. The expectation is that heads will provide a school with professional educational leadership. They are expected not only to administer the school but to give it a direction. The determination of the curriculum and a variety of curriculum-related activities involves the head in a professional function which is not that of class teaching. Thus many potential conflicts in the schools are not between bureaucracy and professionality but between competing professional judgments. In the vignette of the conflict between Mr Dingle and his head, although it is too brief to capture the nature of the professional dispute, it is nevertheless implicit. We cannot deny the head's professionality. This is his source of influence and, as we have seen, his power emanates from this professional influence backed by his professional authority.

A third point is that the model does not explicitly take account of one source of power available to teachers as a group which is trade union power. The fact that it is not considered does not mean that it is easy to conceptualise. It is less easy still to demonstrate its significance. Corwin was not oblivious to this aspect of power in schools. Indeed, he is the author of one of the key American studies of *militant professionalism* (Corwin, 1970).

The concept of *militant professionalism*, which involves the notion of teachers confronting the administration on the basis of their professionality, does not cover the problem of unionism, at least as far as British schools are concerned. However, adequate consideration of this question is beyond the scope of this chapter and only the bare outlines of the issue can be considered. Basically it is a question of how far unionism (interest of members) and professionality (interest of clients) converge. One argument stresses total convergence: 'What's good for the teachers is good for the pupils'. Thus when teachers are pressing for improvements in pay, conditions, autonomy, etc. their arguments are couched in terms of the ultimate interests of the pupils. One can be cynical and assume that arguments about the interests of clients are really about the interests of teachers. On the other hand, it is very difficult to deny that what is in the interests of teachers *is* to some degree in the interests of pupils. The present writer has made the distinction of *professionalism* (i.e. the improvement of the professional status, pay and conditions of teachers) and *professionality* (i.e. improvement in the quality of service to clients (Hoyle, 1974). However, although the conceptual difference might have some validity, empirically it is difficult to distinguish between these two elements. If one equates what I have called professionalism with unionism, then we have the basis of an alternative source of power for teachers individually and collectively. The British tradition has been for questions about the conditions of work for teachers to be pressed at national level by teacher's unions combining professional rhetoric with union strategy. Schools as such have not been unionised. Even now militancy in individual schools is an element in a national strategy rather than a school strategy. It does not involve a conflict, although some heads might conceptualise it as such, between teachers and head. However, there are examples where a dispute between head and staff is transformed into a dispute between the head and one or more teachers' unions. In these instances teachers have power, but it is a form of power which fits only into the authority-influence distinction which was made above. The precise nature of this power, and the authority which may or may not underpin it, is a matter for exploration through studies of the relatively rare cases of its occurrence.

The context for the exercise of teachers' professionality is the classroom where by virtue of their knowledge, skill and associated status, they are technically in authority over their pupils, although this authority may, of course, be challenged by pupils. The question of the degree of autonomy enjoyed by the teacher in the exercise of this authority was discussed above. Although the head probably has the legal authority to control the exercise of professional expertise in the classroom and thus the potential power to reduce the teacher's autonomy, in practice this authority remains latent and the teacher by and large does enjoy a relatively high degree of autonomy. There are a number of reasons for this. One is the aforementioned reluctance of the heads to utilise and make overt their legal authority. A second is the heads' recognition of the limitations of their own expertise, especially in subject areas at the secondary level. A third is the strong professional norm of non-interference in the teacher's classroom activities. A fourth is the sheer difficulty of exercising control over teachers since their work is carried out in private settings and is hard to evaluate, especially in the short term.

There is an asymmetry in the exercise of authority by head and teacher. Broadly speaking the head has a high degree of authority in relation to school policy, curriculum and organisation but an authority over classroom practice limited by the factors noted above which, in effect, bestow a considerable degree of autonomy on the teacher. On the other hand, although the teacher has enjoyed a reasonably high degree of *de facto* authority over classroom practice, the teacher's *de jure* and *de facto* authority in relation to school policy, curriculum and organisation are limited. This asymmetry is particularly true of the primary school; in the secondary school it is, of course, modified because of the greater distribution of authority over policy and curricular matters via the staff hierarchy. However, changes have been taking place in the exercise of authority in school which have given teachers a greater opportunity to participate in decision-making over matters of policy, curriculum and organisation. This represents a shift towards *collegial authority*, the pattern of authority which is held to be appropriate to organisations which are staffed by professionals.

The interacting spheres model

Although the professional-bureaucratic distinction serves a useful heuristic purpose in identifying a potential source of conflict in schools, in practice, because head teachers need the support of their staff and teachers will normally prefer to avoid conflicts with their heads, a pattern of accommodation prevails. Lortie identified a *balance* between authority and control. There are at least two ways of conceptualising this balance. One is through a functionist perspective which holds that there is an inherent equilibrium between the authority of the head and the autonomy of the teacher. From this point of view a recognition by both parties of the 'good of the school' leads to a natural limitation on over-centralisation over-independence. Although there *are* conflicts, the 'hidden hand' of pupil welfare assures that homeostasis is maintained. But, as noted in Chapter 1, both conflict theorists and phenomenologists would challenge this cosy assumption. An alternative view, though it is not wholly incompatible with the functionalist approach, is the action approach which would see both sets of participants as negotiating an accommodation. In a seminal study of the hospital as an organisation, Anselm Strauss (1963) noted that 'professionals and non-professionals are implicated in a great web of negotiation', the outcome of which he summarised as a *negotiated order*.

Hanson (1976), in a study of three schools in Silverwood, an American school district, observed the same process of negotiation. He reports that these negotiation processes have a degree of predictability and that there exist certain rules of the game. He delineates what he termed the *Interacting Spheres Model*. Using Lortie's concept of *zone*, he identified a separate zone for administrators and for teachers which each party recognised as legitimate. The teachers' zone was essentially occupied by 'instructional decisions'. The administrators' zone was occupied by four decision areas: security, allocation, boundary and evaluation. However, the two zones overlapped and it was in the area of overlap that the negotiations occurred. Each party used direct and indirect strategies to manage the members of the other sphere and each used defensive strategies to protect their own sphere from outside intervention.

Collegial authority

The hypothesised bureaucratic-professional conflict is predicated on the assumption that the forms of authority underpinning each are incompatible. However, another view suggests that there is a form of authority appropriate to professionally-staffed organisations which subsumes the professionality of administration and the professionality of practice, i.e. teaching and tasks associated with teaching, such as curriculum planning, in the case of schools, since it entails collective responsibility for both tasks. This form is *collegial authority*.

Weber identified and named collegial authority as a pattern which differed from bureaucratic authority, but did not develop this concept to any degree. Nor did he explore the implicit conflict between these two forms of authority. Lortie (1964) has defined collegial authority as that in which professional equals govern their affairs through democratic procedures. It is widely held in the literature on organisations and professions that collegial authority is the form most functional for professionally-staffed organisations, since this ensures that the use of expertise is not inhibited by bureaucracy and hierarchy. However, schools are not characterised by collegial authority. Although one could, in theory, construct a variety of models of collegial authority, the following will perhaps suffice to indicate what might be some of its features (Hoyle, 1972):

1 Teachers would integrate their work on a team basis.
2 The teams would have internal democracy and leadership would be variable or rotating.
3 The teams would determine their objectives in the light of school goals.
4 School goals would be determined by a collegium in which all professional members of staff would participate.
5 The chairmanship of the collegium would be the chief executive role.
6 The collegium would have an administrative staff.
7 Evaluation of teacher performance would be by fellow professionals.

This model, or variants of it, would initially appear to have an appeal for teachers since it would guarantee direct teacher participation on an authoritative basis in the decision-making process of the school. However, there are some impediments to the achievement of this model and we can explore some of these. First of all we can consider barriers to the implementation of such a model. One major barrier is the present investiture of legal authority in the head. The demand for accountability would probably ensure resistance to any change in this locus of authority from the head to the collegium. This is not insurmountable. Universities are collegial organisations wherein this legal problem has ostensibly been resolved, although it has to be admitted that the recent need to make staff cuts and other economies in universities has led to disputes over the locus of authority. It is quite possible to invest legal authority in the *collegium* with the incumbent chairperson having a special and identified responsibility. However, this would mean that the chairperson, whose own views could presumably be voted down, might be placed in a position of responsibility without authority and would thus be in a weaker position and would have to resort to various modes of influence to a greater degree than would the head. Insofar as collegial authority entails the acceptance of the collective will of professional equals, this might not be acceptable to the wider society and its political representatives. It would also require a flow of able people who would be willing to accept the position of chairperson without ultimate legal authority.

An associated problem is that of the present differentials in teachers' salaries. Collegiality in its pure form is predicated upon professional equals presumably enjoying equality of remuneration. At present the teaching profession in Britain is stratified into a number of status levels which are linked to different points on the salary scale. Thus, insofar as collegiality was assumed to be based on a common salary scale with automatic increments for length of service only, this would involve a dismantling of the present salary structure, a move which would undoubtedly generate considerable resistance. If, as seems likely, salary differentials are to remain, it is difficult to see what would be their basis if not differences in authority or responsibility which would undermine the principle of collegiality. Those with higher salaries or status would assume, or perhaps have thrust upon them, the power to make decisions. This would presumably remain the case if salary differentials were agreed collegially, i.e. if salaries were a function of peer rating and peer agreement. There is considerable resistance in education to peer rating and it is therefore unlikely that this interpretation of collegiality would be acceptable to teachers.

The institutionalisation of collegial authority in a school is likely to result in a number of ironies. Four can be identified. One is that collegial authority could result in the closer control over the individual teacher's work than the mixed model, and perhaps even more than the bureaucratic model. The essence of collegiality is shared authority, collaborativeness, and peer control. It can operate at a number of levels. At the level of policy-making it entails, as indicated, a *collegium* wherein policy-making in relation to curriculum, organisation, pastoral care, etc. can be exercised. At the level of planning it involves groups of teachers concerned with a particular aspect of the curriculum meeting to determine syllabuses, course materials, models of evaluation, etc. And at the level of pedagogy it involves one of the many varieties of team teaching. In each case collegiality functions to limit the teacher's autonomy. This is most clearly pronounced at the pedagogical level. Lortie (1964) has discussed this problem with considerable insight. Insofar as the team functions as a *small group* – using this term in its quasi-technical sense – and develops shared understandings, common objectives, an agreed division of labour, rotating leadership, etc. the satisfaction to be derived from operating professionally on such a team out-weighs the loss of autonomy. But, as Lortie notes, it is quite possible for teams to become hierarchical, whereupon the individual teacher may have yielded classroom autonomy for an even closer hierarchical control of his or her work than under a bureaucratic system, with a consequent loss of satisfaction. Although this irony is most pronounced at the pedagogical level, it appertains at the other two levels. There is a cost to collegiality which is the loss of some freedom of action. It would remain to be seen whether this loss was outweighed by consequent gains in the collective control of the professional activities of a group of colleagues.

A second irony arises from the fact that collegiality can generate a decision-making context which can be construed as having some of the characteristics of bureaucracy. Collegiality generates committees, meetings and documentation which, although they are not necessarily components of the ideal type of bureaucracy, nevertheless conform to the familiar negative connotation of time-consuming activities which divert energies from the core task. The problem is that even at the school level, or at least the level of the larger secondary school, policy and planning tasks cannot be undertaken in detail by the *collegium*. This work has to be devolved to committees, working parties, etc. Committee structures of this kind generate an ambivalence amongst teachers in quasi-collegial schools. On the one hand they welcome participation in decision-making, although, as we shall see in the next section, in some areas rather more than others. On the other hand they resent the time which they are required to spend on these activities which they often see as detracting from the core task of teaching or spending many hours out of school time. Whether this resentment is a function of the fact that schools can, at the present time, only be quasi-collegial, and therefore teachers feel that they are undertaking tasks 'which the head gets paid for', or whether they would not experience this resentment in a system which was wholly collegial, would remain to be seen.

A third irony of collegiality is what has been termed 'the receding locus of power' (Noble and Pym, 1970). In bureaucratic and structurally loose systems there is no doubt where power (i.e. authority) lies. It lies with the head and is delegated through the hierarchy. In a collegial system authority is diffuse. It appears not to lie with committees but somehow *between* committees. Noble and Pym write:

> In complex organisations in the spheres of education, industry, administration or commerce, this Kafkaesque experience is very common; wherever or at whatever level one applies to the organisation, the 'real' decisions always seem to be taken somewhere else. The lower level officials or committees argue that they, of course, can only make recommendations. Departments must seek the approval of inter-departmental committees, these in turn can only submit reports and recommendations to the general management committee. It is there we were told that decisions must be made.
>
> At the higher level one finds a different situation. At the very top, the fiduciary board was a formal 'rubber stamp'; at the level of the executive board decisions were of a very general and very long run nature and a policy of non-interference in the details of management was adhered to. In the general management committee, however, though votes are taken and decisions formally reached there was a widespread feeling, not infrequently expressed even by some of its senior members, of powerlessness, a feeling that decisions were really taken elsewhere.

Thus, in a collegial system there is the frustration of not knowing where power lies and *in having nobody to blame*.

A fourth irony is implicit in the assumption that collegiality enhances the prospect of innovation. In the classic bureaucracy v. professionality distinction, bureaucracy is held to exert a constraint on innovation. As long ago as 1935 one writer concluded: 'The bureaucrat governs his actions by rules and precedent and obstructs needed change. The professional man governs his actions in the light of science and learning and is investive' (Chapin, 1935, quoted Corwin, 1965). Although it is the case that collegiality is conducive to innovation, under certain circumstances it can be obstructive to change. These circumstances would be where the *collegium* consisted of a series of self-negating veto groups which, in defence of particular interest, were prepared to block the proposed innovations of others. Thus, although the bureaucrat is orientated to seeing the problems and finding reasons why something 'cannot be done', the collegium could consist of inverted Micawbers, always 'waiting for something to turn down'.

Thus there is, potentially, a number of ironies inherent in the concept of collegiality. It may well be, however, that these ironies can be identified only because collegiality is viewed from a situation in which it does not exist. However, were collegiate systems to be created, these problems could well be resolved in practice. What we have at the moment is a system wherein schools have a distinct locus of authority but, for a number of reasons, the heads in whom this authority resides often seek to create a quasi-collegial system. Thus collegiality is not inherent in the system but is a function of leadership style whereby teachers are given the opportunity to participate in the decision-making process by benevolent heads rather than as of right.

Patterns for interaction

Pressures towards greater teacher participation have stemmed from four sources: the changes in the socio-political climate of the 1960s, the growing need for greater teacher collaboration at the levels of power, planning and pedagogy arising from curriculum change, the growing complexity of secondary schools which has undermined the one-man-band kind of leadership, and the growth of courses in educational management which have emphasised participative approaches. Although the general term *participation* was used in the 1960s and 1970s and is being retained in this section, it has been frequently pointed out that in most schools *consultation* is the more accurate description, at least for the situation in state schools.

In state schools, and indeed in independent schools, the locus of responsibility has not shifted from the head. Neither LEAs, boards of governors nor trustees have been inclined to bestow responsibility on a collective. Thus patterns of participation have been determined by the structures established by heads as the result of personal beliefs, of staff pressure or both. In a well-known paper, Tannenbaum and Schmidt (1958) set out the range of possibilities as shown in Figure 3 opposite.

This is a useful model, but two points can be made. One is that it is a linear scale and thus carries the implicit assumption that a particular form of participation is appropriate for all decisions. In fact, it may well be the case that different points on the scale are appropriate to particular kinds of decision. For example, it might be that a high level of teacher participation is appropriate in relation to curricular decisions, but inappropriate to decisions over matters of school routine. Thus this scale would be more usefully plotted against the different sorts of decisions which need to be taken. A second point is that the title of the paper from which the diagram comes implies that the head *can* choose his or her own style. In this connection one has to say that what the diagram illustrates is essentially a set of alternative *structures* rather than *styles*. The distinction between these two concepts is difficult to sustain in any clear way, but style is the more embracing concept covering the nature of all the leadership acts undertaken by the head amongst which are the establishment of structures-for-interaction (Halpin, 1966), the structures which the head creates for handling decision-making and communication.

Although the head retains authority at all pointt of the Tannenbaum and Schmidt continuum, a number of problems are associated with the more 'liberal' patterns. One is that the pattern adopted by the head should be compatible with the expectations of teachers. It cannot be assumed that all teachers would wish to participate in the decision-making process, especially if the structures serve to mask the reality of their limited capacity to affect policies. Teachers vary considerably in their desire for participation and, as Alutto and Belasco (1972) have shown, this varies by age, sex, socio-economic status and marital status. Moreover, where teachers wish to participate this wish does not apply equally to all kinds of decision. For example, a study of this fact in eight British schools, primary and secondary (Conway, 1978) found that teachers desired most

Figure 3 (adapted from Tannenbaum, R. and Schmidt, W. W. (1958) 'How to choose a leadership pattern', *Harvard Business Review*, 51(3))

head-centred leadership							subordinate-centred leadership
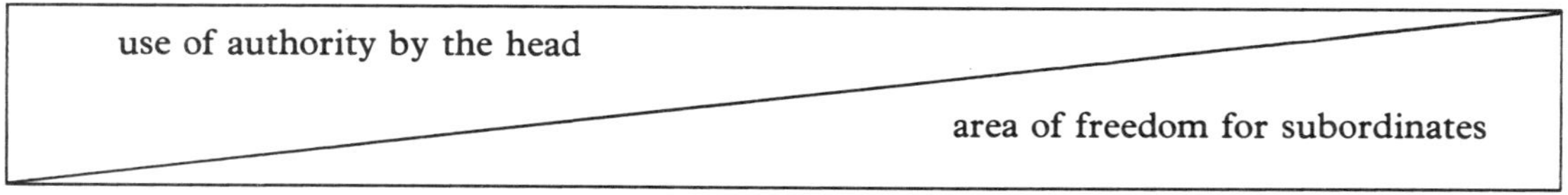 use of authority by the head					area of freedom for subordinates		
head makes decision and announces it	head 'sells' decision	head presents ideas and invites questions	head presents tentative decision subject to change	head presents problem, gets suggestions, makes decision	head defines limits, asks group to make decision	head permits subordinates to function within limits defined by supervisor	

strongly to participate in decisions about, for example, textbook selection, pupil problems and teaching methods but least strongly in the issue of staff grievances, community problems and administrative staff problems. By and large, their desires were matched by their actual involvement. The greatest mismatch was in the appointment of staff where teachers desired high, but experienced only low, participation.

A second problem arises from the fact that participation can fulfil different functions which are not always compatible. The creation of a decision-making structure which is both conducive to the efficient running of the school and meets the teachers' desire for participation is a complex task. Dill (1964) has usefully pointed out that participation can have different and competing goals:

1 *Control goal* Ensure that decisions do get made and that, for control purposes, there is someone to talk with when it comes time to evaluate decisions or seek explanations for their results.
2 *Motivation goal* Bridge the gap that often exists between making and implementing decisions by making them in ways that make people who will have to help carry them out feel identified with their successful implementation.
3 *Quality goal* Improve the quality of decisions by involving those who will have most to contribute to the decisions.
4 *Training goal* Develop skills for handling problems in the men who will move eventually into administrative positions, and test for the presence of these skills.
5 *Efficiency goal* Get decisions made as quickly and with as little waste of manpower as possible.

As Dill notes:

> Goals 1 and 5 might be said to argue for fairly limited participation in decision-making. Goals 2, 3 and 4 argue for more extensive participation—but in different ways: 2 for participation by the people who may be affected by the decision; 3 for particulation by the people who are expert in solving it; and 4 for participation by people who may be neither personally involved nor expert, but who are being prepared for advancement.

A third problem arises from the possibility of a discrepancy between *organisational structures* and *leadership style*. The distinction, though rather crude, is worth making because it is possible for a head to establish a decision-making structure which is incompatible with an overall leadership style. A typical problem of this kind occurred not infrequently in the 1960s and 1970s when heads, under pressure to establish more participative structures, did so and later found that they were temperamentally or conceptually incapable of working effectively within a more open system and regressed to a more authoritarian style which was out of kilter with the structure, or alternatively sought to achieve their preferred ends by micropolitical processes within the interstices of the structures.

These problems have to be resolved through a continuing process of negotiation. A blueprint representation of structures does not help one to understand just how participatory forms work in practice, yet sustained and detailed accounts of this process are rare. One such study of this process in a British school is Elizabeth Richardson's (1973) detailed account of the pattern of participation at Nailsea School. The school was initially a grammar school which became a comprehensive school under the same head, Denys John, who addressed himself, and encouraged his colleagues to address themselves, both to the new problems which comprehensivisation generated and to the ways in which staff members might participate in policies which tackled these problems. The study illuminates how John negotiated, and continued to re-negotiate, an optimum balance between his legal authority, his own beliefs about the purposes of a comprehensive school, his leadership style, the aspirations towards participation amongst the staff which he encouraged, the professional skills of the staff, and their beliefs about the purposes of education. The study demonstrates that participation is a *process*, the continuous redefinition of structures and relationships.

The Tannenbaum and Schmidt model does not include some of the more radical approaches to participation. These emerged initially in such independent schools as Summerhill and Dartington long before the changes in the socio-political climate of the 1960s. The impetus came from the pedagogical beliefs of educationists like A. S. Neill which would be incompatible with any but a fully participative pattern of decision-making involving pupils as well as staff. Radical modes of participation were adopted in the free schools which flourished in North America and, to a lesser degree in Britain, in the 1960s. Within the state system in Britain, Countesthorpe was the school which became best known for its participative pattern. The innovative characteristics of the school were briefly discussed in Chapter 2. Tim McMullen had a strong belief that the curricular and pedagogical innovations envisaged could best be achieved through a participatory pattern of school government. The pattern established was described as following in a General Statement endorsed by the Moot in 1973.

> The moot and the community council formulate the College's policy. The principal, as well as playing a full part in policy-making through the moot, the committees and the community council, acts with his deputies as chief executive. In the light of existing LEA practice the moot recognises the special responsibilities of the principal representing the College to the outside world, in particular the governors, the LEA and the local community. The moot is open to all staff, students in so far as they wish to attend, and parents when they are able. The community council is a body representing each class or group of users within the adult and youth provision of the College. The moot meets about once a month and the community council about once a term.
>
> The moot forms sub-committees, standing, or ad hoc, to deal with specific business. The principal standing committee meets once a week to consider points at issue to advise the executive, set up its own working parties and to determine when a matter affecting basic policy requires a moot to be called. The principal and deputies attend all meetings to give and take advice. The day-to-day business of the school is undertaken as appropriate by the principal, deputies, the administrator, the staff as tutors, year-teachers and heads of departments. (Watts, 1977)

In his discussion of the place of the head in participative government, John Watts, the second Warden of Countesthorpe, writes most illuminatingly of his role. Although policy decisions were made by the Moot in which he had only had one independent vote, it would seem that as head he retained a considerable influential voice. His role as executive afforded an important basis for such influence. Although in conventional political theory legislative and executive functions are differentiated, accounts of political practice invariably reveal the constraining power of the latter. As the chief executive, Watts had access to information which was not necessarily available to the rest of the staff, an important source of influence. Moreover, as head, Watts was the person in direct contact with outside agencies and thus both received 'messages' from the outside world to which he sensitised the staff and conveyed to them the political realities of the outside world. Finally, the head's influence functioned through an acceptance by the staff of his professional authority based on his knowledge, skills and experience. However, there remains the potential conflict between the head who retains legal authority and the body in which it has invested decision-making powers. Of this problem Watts writes as follows:

> The problem that most often is raised for me by others is that of possible conflict between head and moot. This is an obvious one only because conflict between head and staff is normal: even under a liberal headship they advise and consent, while he consults and decides. But the participatory system depends upon an initial agreement of aims. That is why it is very doubtful whether an existing school could go over to a participatory approach. I wouldn't recommend it. Countesthorpe was made possible by the first head's clear announcement of intention which enabled him to recruit a staff who wanted to work in that way. With head and staff agreed on basics, then conflicts can be resolved by open discussion in reference to them, provided all parties learn to tolerate conflict, use it to identify issues and make compromises in order to reach consensus. (Watts, 1977)

A case of conflict in an embryonic participative system occurred at William Tyndale. The head, Terry Ellis, told the Inquiry, which considered the problems at the school (Auld, 1976) that he was firmly of the view that the educational aims and teaching methods of the school should be determined by the teaching staff as a whole. This was initially welcomed by all staff members but in the first term of the new dispensation, according to the Report of the Inquiry, only one collective decision of any consequence was taken. This concerned the adaptation of a reading scheme but, in fact, the decision was never implemented. Instead of collective agreement, divisions of opinion on the staff became polarised. The head and four members of staff remained committed to radical innovations in curriculum and methods. Four other members of staff were resistant to these innovations, and of these one was so strident in her opposition that in the view of the Inquiry, her opposition became counter-productive and she lost the support of the other teachers who shared her views. This teacher later publicised her criticism of developments in the school to outside bodies. The head was thus in a dilemma. The teaching approach which was favoured by himself and by some of his colleagues was opposed by others and consensus was unattainable. On the other hand, the imposition of uniformity did not accord with his beliefs. The Report of the Inquiry stated:

> To achieve uniformity throughout the School in teaching policies and methods, Mr Ellis had either to apply himself to bringing the Staff to some basis for a common approach or, failing that, to put his own mark as Headteacher on the overall teaching policies and methods of the School. He did neither. (Auld, 1976)

Here the Report would seem to overestimate the possibility and desirability of imposing teaching methods in what is ultimately a loosely-coupled system. Swidler (1979) studied two free schools in Berkeley, California functioning in the 1970s. 'Group High' had two hundred students who were mainly white, middle class and from well-educated liberal families. School staff and students were committed to a negotiated curriculum which would enable students to better understand themselves and their social context and to a relationship between teacher and student based on equality. Staff and students at 'Ethnic High' were multiracial and their relationship was also based on equality. The curriculum was negotiated but there was a specific commitment to a multicultural content. Both schools disposed of the usual authority relationship. The leader was elected by both staff and students, decisions were democratically taken by both groups within the 'collectives' and within the school as a whole on such matters as policy, staffing, expenditure and individual cases. There was much discussion about the purposes of the school and about the characters of both teachers and students. The interest groups met in large areas of the school building rather than in formal classrooms. The schools were largely 'protected' from the normal external administrative controls.

The study was concerned with the way in which the schools functioned without formal authority. Teachers had to rely on charisma and on establishing close personal relationships with students. This generated a considerable degree of strain amongst the teachers and turnover was high. A considerable amount of time was spent discussing the school, its curriculum and relationships in sessions lasting up to two and a half days. The special mission of the school replaced formal authority as the mechanism of integration. The underlying dynamics of the two organisations were shaped by the tension between cohesion and disintegration. Cohesion had to be achieved through the personal influence of teachers which gave the group a sense of commitment and solidarity. But with charisma at a premium, decline in the influence of the teachers led to the emergence of conflicts and non-cooperation. Although the two schools were to an extent protected from the influence of their socio-political environments they could not be wholly insulated, and environmental pressures contributed to the instability of the two schools.

The dilemmas of radical patterns of participation are reviewed in the above cases. The odds against success are high. One major problem is the relatively hostile environment which has always existed even in the relatively participative *Zeitgeist* of the 1960s. Another is the universal and timeless tension between the individual and the group in the specific context of a loosely-coupled system. A third is the dilemma of leadership whereby the head who is committed both to participative decision-making and progressive schooling has to yield on one principle or the other if consensus cannot be achieved. As John Watts points out, the best chance of sustaining these two principles occurs in a new school which can recruit staff who share these commitments.

Conclusion

This chapter has focused on the distribution of power in the school particularly between the head and the teachers. A number of potential conflicts appear to be inherent in the school, the most basic of which is that which occurs between the legal authority of the head and the professional authority of teachers. In terms of organisational theory this translates into a question of the balance between control and autonomy. At the political level it translates into a balance between two forms of power, the legal authority of the head and resources of influence of the teacher—though the head too has highly significant resources of influence. At the level of management theory it translates into the structure for participation which heads establish as a function of their leadership style and teachers' responses to these structures.

Potential conflicts appear to become explicit and serious in only relatively rare instances. For the most part there is a recognition that although the head has substantial legal power, this remains for the most part confined to certain policy areas and that the teachers are left free to exercise their professional skills in a relatively independent zone of teaching styles and strategies. However, this neatly functionalist manifestation of balance is always potentially fragile and the overlap between these zones a perennially contested area. There are a number of instances in the literature where conflict has become acute when the balance has been seriously disturbed. The potential for disturbance would seem to be highest in the more collegial schools, though there are instances where a high handed authoritarian stance on the part of the head has led to severe conflict. The risks are higher in a collegial setting because, where the buffer zone is removed, the number of mechanisms for minimising conflict disappear. In the absence of a true *collegium*, a situation which the existing law and external expectations preclude, the head either successfully carries a fully-participating staff or fails to do so thus creating a situation of direct conflict.

Although there is sufficient commonality of structure between schools, at least schools of the same type, to permit generalisations to be made about authority structures, each school will also generate a relatively distinctive configuration of power relationship which is alternately the outcome of the leadership style adopted by the head and the response of the staff and the micro-political activities of head and staff members. These two aspects will be the focus of Chapters 5 and 6.

5 Leadership and Mission

> Just as Rome once had Fabius as the best leader in times requiring that the war be drawn out, so later she had Scipio in times suitable for winning it
>
> MACHIAVELLI *Discourses*

This chapter explores a neglected aspect of the role of the head, that of identifying a 'mission' for the school. There are perhaps two main reasons for this neglect. One is that it is a somewhat diffuse activity which is rooted in a person's stance towards educational issues and conveyed via language and actions of a symbolic kind rather than through clearly identifiable tasks. It is not amenable therefore to research in the conventional mode. The other reason is that the notion of 'mission' smacks of a discredited approach to leadership, the heroic 'man on horseback' image which is certainly at odds with the ideas of educational leadership which emerged in the 1960s whereby a head is seen as *primus inter pares* in a collegial system and perhaps more a servant of the teachers, facilitating their professional activities, than inducing a commitment to a particular vision.

The role of the head has certainly changed in recent years. It has become overloaded with expectations to the point at which, were heads to seek to meet them all, they would risk the burn-out which is affecting so many. One of the dilemmas of the head is to select from the range and diversity of expectations those to which they should give most time and attention. We have a good idea of what school leaders actually *do* from the growing number of studies which have sampled their activities (e.g. Wolcott, 1983; O'Dempsey, 1976; Peterson, 1976; Willis, 1980; Martin and Willower, 1981; Sproull, 1981). These studies not only illuminate the diversity of the tasks of heads but how, typically, these change with great rapidity if not from minute to minute then from quarter hour to quarter hour. No doubt many of the actions of these heads are concerned with building a mission for their schools, but the diffuse nature of this task means that it is implicit in the welter of specific tasks which heads constantly undertake in response to the immediate and contingent. One critic (Gronn, 1983) has dubbed this line of research 'neo-Taylorism' for its time-and-motion assumptions, a view rejected by another contributor (Willower, 1983).

By and large, management theory and research do not engage with this aspect of the role of head because their focus is largely on the management of personnel and resources rather than the more elusive idiographic and inspirational aspects of the role. Some recent developments in the theory and practice of school management such as school-based curriculum development, school-focused in-service training and the self evaluation of schools (Bolam, 1982; Dalin and Rust, 1983; McMahon, 1986) are putting a premium, perhaps for the first time, on the public clarification of a mission for each school. Conventional research offers little guide as to how heads have in the past sought to construct and convey a mission nor how they might do so.

This issue of educational leadership as involving the identification of a mission for the school is a highly problematic and tendentious issue. Nevertheless, it is an issue which is in need of further discussion. It is the purpose of this chapter to put it on the agenda.

School leaders: managers, politicians, philosophers

The study of educational leadership is embedded in management theory which, in turn, has its intellectual roots in social psychology. In spite of much excellent work in this field, which will be briefly reviewed in the next section, there is something missing. One element in this 'something' is relatively easily identified. It is that mangement theories of leadership are apolitical or, at least, leave the political element implicit. Organisations are characterised by micropolitical activity and leadership is to a considerable degree a political task. There is an increasing consciousness of this aspect of educational leadership and micropolitics is the topic of the next chapter.

However, having added the political dimension, there is still something else missing. For other academic approaches to leadership one has to go to history and political studies—macropolitics this time. However, one has mainly to infer the qualities of leaders from studies of the historical and political circumstances in which they manifest themselves or from biographies. It would seem that the 'something' is the leader's capacity to grasp the configuration of forces at work in the environment, to construct an achievable mission – the art of the possible – to convey this mission to others often through the skilful use of language and symbol, and to attain a commitment to the mission.

To suggest that theories of school leadership should incorporate these charismatic, even heroic, aspects of leadership may be seen as pure bathos. It would certainly fuel staffroom humour about school leadership. To imagine that the thousands of school leaders might be touched by the heroic is rather absurd. Certainly the present writer has deep reservations about 'the man-on-horseback' approach to leadership. And yet effective school leadership depends, even in situations in which school policies are centralised, on the capacity of the head to articulate a mission for the school.

Consideration of leadership has recently been enhanced by the philosophical approach of Hodgkinson (1983) whose work will be used as a resource at various points in this chapter. His basic taxonomy is reproduced in Figure 4, over. He writes:

> Within this scheme the ideal typical sequences is as follows. Organisational values are articulated by top level administration through philosophical processes (argument, dialectic, logic, rhetoric and value clarification). This is the level of *idea*. The idea emergent from this first phase must be translated into some sort of plan and reduced to a written, persisting and communicable form. This form must then be entered into a political process of persuasion. This is the domain of power, resource, control and politics, and we have moved from the level of ideas to the level of *people*. Coalitions must be formed, levers pulled, persons persuaded as power and support are marshalled around the project or plan. Each of these three process phases of administration can be subsumed under the rubric of policy-making.
>
> When power is aligned and resources are committed, the next stage (still a *people* stage) requires the mobilisation and organising of what economists call the factors of production – land, labour and capital – around the organisational purposes. This phase is critical and involves, metaphorically speaking, a shift of gears from the

Figure 4 (from Hodgkinson, C. (1983) *The Philosophy of Leadership*, Blackwell)

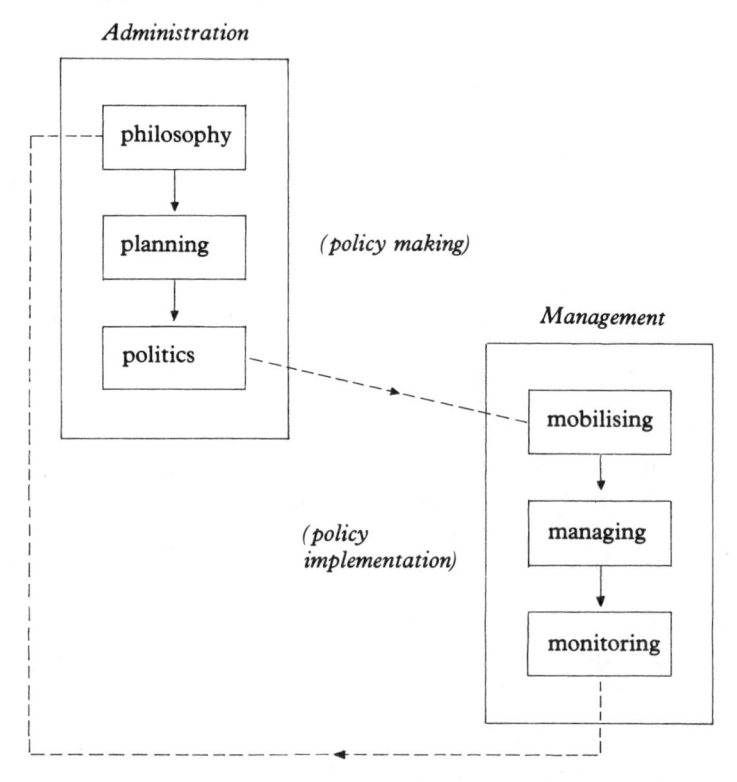

```
Administration
┌─────────────────────────────┐
│   ┌──────────────┐          │
│   │  philosophy  │          │
│   └──────┬───────┘          │
│          ▼                  │
│   ┌──────────────┐   (policy making)
│   │  planning    │          │
│   └──────┬───────┘          │
│          ▼                  │         Management
│   ┌──────────────┐          │  ┌─────────────────────┐
│   │  politics    │─ ─ ─ ─ ─ ┼─▶│  ┌──────────────┐   │
│   └──────────────┘          │  │  │  mobilising  │   │
│                             │  │  └──────┬───────┘   │
│             (policy         │  │         ▼           │
│          implementation)    │  │  ┌──────────────┐   │
│                             │  │  │  managing    │   │
│                             │  │  └──────┬───────┘   │
│                             │  │         ▼           │
│                             │  │  ┌──────────────┐   │
│                             │  │  │  monitoring  │   │
│                             │  │  └──────────────┘   │
└─────────────────────────────┘  └─────────────────────┘
```

administrative into the managerial phase. This phase is an intermediate one of art between the philosophy of policy making on the one hand and the science of management on the other; it is here where, if at all, the pieces are put together and philosophy is moved from the realm of facts, action and *things*.

The taxonomy is valuable in many ways. Firstly, it reaffirms the importance of the *idea* of leadership. Secondly, it recognises and locates the political dimension of leadership. And thirdly, in his extension of the model, Hodgkinson distinguishes between three levels of reality: philosophy and planning which are concerned with *ideas*, politics and mobilising which are tasks involved in achieving a transition from ideas to action and are concerned with *people*, and *managing* and *monitoring* which are concerned with *things*. Current theories of leadership are mainly concerned with people, and to a lesser degree with things. As a prelude to a discussion of the domain of ideas in leadership and the concept of mission, we can briefly review the current state of the art in leadership theory and research.

Theories of leadership

The initial assumption about leadership was that it was a function of personal characteristics — the *trait* approach. However, this approach proved to have little power in predicting effective leadership since it excluded consideration of leadership *style* and the context of leadership. No 'timeless leadership qualities' were satisfactorily identified and effective leadership was seen to be relevant to context. Some *clusters* of effective leadership have been identified (Stogdill, 1948) but it is the exercise of these clusters through a *leadership style* in relation to a particular *context* which is important.

Early work on *leadership style* centred on *democratic, authoritarian* and *laissez faire* styles with the evidence purporting to demonstrate the greater effectiveness of the democratic style. However, these particular concepts were influenced by a prevailing ideology which, in the 1930s and 1940s when many of these studies were carried out, ensured a predeliction for the democratic style of leadership. However, this particular set of concepts was challenged by developments in leadership studies from the 1950s onwards. It was not that authoritarian leadership turned out to be more effective than democratic leadership, but to conceptualise leadership in this way was to miss the point that although *successful* democratic leadership was more effective than successful *authoritarian* leadership, even the latter led to a higher level of effectiveness and satisfaction than *unsuccessful* leadership. Effective leadership in terms of achievement and group satisfaction was the outcome not only of interpersonal relationships, but also of the sense of achievement arising from a task completed.

From the 1950s onwards almost all those undertaking research into leadership identified two key dimensions of leadership: *personal relationships* and *task achievement*. The reader can get a flavour of what aspects of leadership behaviour are entailed in each of these two factors by perusing the following list (a combination of two previous lists: Hanson, 1979a and Hoyle, 1981) which have emerged from independent studies:

Barnard	(1938)	effectiveness	employee orientation
Argyris	(1957)	formal behaviour	individual behaviour
Getzels/ Guba	(1957)	nomothetic	idiographic
Likert	(1961)	restrictive	participative
Bass	(1960)	task effectiveness	interaction effectiveness
Bales	(1951)	instrumental	expressive
Brown	(1967)	system orientated	person orientated
Fiedler	(1965)	task motivated	relationship motivated
Halpin	(1966)	initiating structure	consideration

In short: the effective leader ensures that tasks are accomplished and at the same time colleagues feel that their social needs are being met.

Of these pairs of concepts we will use *initiating structure* and *consideration* because they are the pair which have perhaps been used most frequently in the study of the management of schools. Halpin (1966) defined them as follows:

> *Initiating structure* refers to the leader's behaviour in delineating the relationship between himself and members of his work group; and in endeavouring to establish well-defined patterns of organisation, channels of communication, and methods of procedure.
> *Consideration* refers to behaviour indicative of friendship, mutual trust, respect, and warmth in the relationship between the leader and members of his staff.

The two factors emerged from a tradition of research into leadership based on the Leader Behaviour Discipline Questionnaire (LBDQ). Although many leadership styles have been identified, indicating that there are many roads to effectiveness, the two concepts remain basic to most patterns. Halpin took this research tradition forward to develop a questionnaire for determining the organisational climates of schools, i.e. teachers' perceptions of the behaviour of their principals and of the effects of this behaviour on their own job satisfaction. A first step was to identify four characteristics of principals' behaviour and four characteristics of teachers' behaviour.

1 *Disengagement* refers to the teachers' tendency to be 'not with it'. This dimension describes a group which is 'going through the motions', a group that is 'not in gear' with

respect to the task at hand. It corresponds to the more general concept of *anomie* as first described by Durkheim. In short, this subtest focuses upon the teachers' behaviour in a task-orientated situation.

2 *Hindrance* refers to the teachers' feeling that the principal burdens them with routine duties, committee demands, and other requirements which the teachers construe as unnecessary 'busywork.' The teachers perceive that the principal is hindering rather than facilitating their work.

3 *Esprit* refers to morale. The teachers feel that their social needs are being satisfied, and that they are, at the same time, enjoying a sense of accomplishment in their job.

4 *Intimacy* refers to the teachers' enjoyment of friendly social relations with each other. This dimension describes a social-needs satisfaction which is not necessarily associated with task-accomplishment.

Principal's behaviour;

5 *Aloofness* refers to behaviour by the principal which is characterised as formal and impersonal. He 'goes by the book' and prefers to be guided by rules and policies rather than to deal with the teachers in an informal, face-to-face situation. His behaviour, in brief, is universalistic rather than particularistic, nomothetic rather than idiosyncratic. To maintain this style, he keeps himself – at least, 'emotionally' – at a distance from his staff.

6 *Production emphasis* refers to behaviour by the principal which is characterised by close supervision of the staff. He is highly directive and plays the role of a 'straw boss'. His communication goes in only one direction, and he is not sensitive to feedback from the staff.

7 *Thrust* refers to behaviour by the principal which is characterised by his evident effort in trying to 'move the organisation'. Thrust behaviour is marked not by close supervision, but by the principal's attempt to motivate the teachers through the example which he personally sets. Apparently, because he does not ask the teachers to give of themselves any more than he willingly gives of himself, his behaviour, though starkly task-orientated, is nonetheless viewed favourably by the teachers.

8   *Consideration* refers to behaviour by the principal which is characterised by an inclination to treat the teachers 'humanly', to try to do a little something extra for them in human terms.

The next stage was to combine the responses for each school to yield a school profile and then to establish by factor analysis whether these school scores combined to yield distinctive figurations. He identified six distinctive configurations which he termed *organisational climates* which he labelled: *open, autonomous, controlled, familar, paternal, closed*. The interested reader should consult Halpin (1966) for greater detail of the climates.

Current theories of leadership are still dominated by powerful evidence for the existence of these two key factors. However, two additional elements in prevailing leadership theory are relevant to the argument of this chapter. The first is what has long been known but was for a long time omitted from theoretical formulations, which is that effective leadership is context based. Tannenbaum, Weischler and Massarik (1961) noted that the effective leader takes into account four sets of forces when deciding what actions to take. These are: forces in the leader, forces in subordinates, forces in the situation (e.g. type of organisation, the nature of the task and the availability of time) and forces in the environment (this latter aspect was added after reflection on earlier work, see Tannenbaum and Schmidt, 1958). The inclusion of the context in which leadership is exercised is referred to as the *contingency theory of leadership* which is related to the contingency theory of management discussed in Chapter 2. Perhaps the best known on such theory is that developed and tested by Fiedler (1965). However, although Fielder's work takes account of context, it is the immediate work-group context which is dominant and the emphasis remains on forces in the leader and forces in subordinates. The *path-goal theory of leadership* (House, 1971; House and Dessler, 1974) emphasises the importance of leadership behaviour which encourages realistic and positive expectations amongst subordinates and provides structures for their attainment. It also emphasises the point that effective leadership styles will vary with context and that the leader must match style to context, what Getzels and Guba (1957) earlier termed a *transactional style*. However, the path-goal theory remains largely concerned with the immediate work-group, the authority system and the task as the contextual factors, with the task being largely conceptualised in limited and immediate terms. As Hanson (1979b) points out, contingency theories of leadership have received little application to educational contexts. He also very rightly notes that even contingency theories and research have, in fact, paid relatively little attention to the socio-political context outside the organisation and suggests the need for an open-systems perspective on leadership, a point to which we will return later in this chapter.

A second development in leadership theory which is relevant to the present discussion is the identification of a third dimension in relation to the basic *task* and *person* dimensions. It is hardly surprising that additional factors have been 'discovered'. Indeed, a number of the writers listed above as having identified the two basic factors have added to them without invalidating in any way the basic duality. However, one such addition is particularly interesting. Yukl (1975) adds to Halpin's *initiating structure* and *consideration* a third factor: *decision-centralisation*, i.e. the degree of leader influence over group decisions, the participative dimension. The potential significance of this dimension can be seen in the work of Nias (1980) which showed that the *de*-centralisation of decisions did not necessarily increase the job satisfaction of teachers. In fact, the teachers in her sample generally responded well to what Nias calls *positive leadership* but negatively both to passive and Bourbon (i.e. authoritarian) leadership. Teachers' responses similarly indicated a desire for 'common goals', 'continuity', 'consistency', 'direction', 'coherent philosophy' and 'priorities'. She writes:

> Implicitly, therefore, the head is expected to take a lead in establishing aims for his school. When he did so, this behaviour received appreciative comment from his teachers. Typical comments about 'positive' heads were: 'The headteacher set the direction of the school. He was an old-fashioned patriarch in many ways, but the staff were an open group, and the fact that the place was full of certainties made it a good place to start in.' 'It's much better at this school. We're given a lead. We're under quite strong pressure from the head to conform in certain ways, but that's better I think than at (his previous school) where you were left entirely to do your own thing.'

Nias's work is based on a relatively small sample and would need much more support before the findings could be regarded as a contribution to leadership theory for schools. Moreover, there needs to be further support for the separate factor of *decision-centralisation* as identified by Yukl since it could be argued that its components are, in effect, a sub-set of the components of Halpin's *initiating structure* factor. Nevertheless, the possibility of a separate factor raises some interesting issues, in particular, the importance to a school of a distinctive and positive 'mission' and for the head to initiate and sustain this 'mission'.

A third development in leadership theory is education-specific and is concerned with the influence of heads on school improvement. Hall and colleagues at the University of Texas have worked on the leadership styles of school principals and Leithwood and colleagues at the Ontario Institute for the Study of Education have worked on principal profiles, detailed descriptions of their behaviour. It would be a misrepresentation of their work to argue that they demonstrate the effective principal as the one who can create a staff commitment to a mission. The data in both cases is far too sophisticated to have imposed on them this global and simplistic notion. However, their findings are not wholly unrelated to the present discussion.

Leithwood and Montgomery (1984) identified four stages of profile 'growth' involving a move from the *administrator* (low) through the *humanitarian* and the *programme manager* to the *problem-solver* (high). The latter, the effective principal, selects goals from a number of public sources, transforms them into short term planning goals and uses them to increase conviction and consistency amongst staff members. This suggests vision, a capacity to analyse and a capacity to motivate. The research suggests that this vision may be pursued in conflict with the views of district administrators. Leithwood and Montgomery (1984) further suggest that a comparison can be made between these 'profiles' and Hall's 'styles' (Hall *et al.*, 1982). Without elaborating or labouring the point, this tradition of research suggests that effective principals fulfil the task and social relations dimensions but transcend their immediate organisational environment in their quest for goals.

> Highly effective principals systematically selected their goals from those espoused for students by agencies of the state, the local school board perceived needs of the community and students served by the school. Because the least effective principals, described by the profile, valued running a smooth ship (administratively) these goals were derived from a sense of the administrative tasks requiring

attention for this to be achieved. Goals did not often spring from curricular, instructional or interpersonal considerations. (Leithwood and Montgomery 1984)

The concept of 'mission'

'Mission' is somewhat vague and is defined in different ways, but, given a particular connotation, it is a useful term to use in relation to the functions of the school. At one end of a possible range of connotations is the military concept of mission. This conveys a highly rational activity. Here mission suggests a clear objective to be achieved within a finite time scale and to which can be attached relatively clear criteria of success. It is very much a technical accomplishment infused with notions of means-ends rationality. At the other end of the hypothesised continuum is the connotation of mission as a process of establishing and maintaining religious faith which may embrace the specific task of conversion duly marked by an appropriate ritual, but is more broadly concerned with the transcendental character of a religion.

The connotation of mission adopted in this chapter lies between the two. It is more than the achievement of a set of specific educational objectives, although these may be encompassed by it. On the other hand it lacks, although some practitioners may seek to equate the two, the ineffable character of a religious mission. The connotation of mission in the present context is of a cluster of goals which the school meets from the range available from the diffuse and diverse range covered by the broad aims of education. Societies establish schools for the purpose of educating the young. However, since education is capable of a variety of interpretations, schools will make their own selection from the range of possible goals. There are two reasons why such a selection is made. One, of course, is the fact that schools cannot do all that is expected of them and even though a constraint on their possible range of goals is imposed from without, there will remain the need to impose further limitations. The other reason is more relevant to the present argument. It is that schools will seek to forge a distinctive identity. Their members like to have a sense of distinctiveness, to feel that their enterprise is somewhat different from that of others. This is noticeable at conferences where teachers tend to speak of their own schools as somehow different from the norm. The 'mission' of the school, then, is the distinctive, or presumed-to-be-distinctive, cluster of goals with associated beliefs, attitudes and activities. This cluster is more than the curriculum of this school where curriculum is narrowly defined in terms of content, but obviously the curriculum in this sense is central and the 'mission' may be generated out of decisions about content. Otherwise, curriculum content will certainly flow from the concept of mission. In practice, concept and content are likely to be the outcome of an interactive process.

There are few organisational theorists whose work contributes to this sort of thinking about organisations, but an important exception is Selznick. In *Leadership and Administration* (1957) he advances the need for organisations to have a mission which he defines broadly as the general aims of the organisation. He points out that an organisational mission cannot be specified in detail nor is it unchanging. He sees it as one of the indispensable tasks of leadership to formulate and present the organisational mission. The importance of the concept of 'mission', despite its lack of specification – inevitable in Selznick's view – can best be understood in the broader context of Selznick's organisational theory. He distinguishes between *organisation* which is 'an expendable tool, a rational instrument engineered to do a job' and an *institution* which is more nearly 'a natural product of social needs and pressures — a responsible and adaptive organism'. Thus organisation is the limited structural and administrative component of the social unit, and institution the global entity including its values. Hence mission relates to the institution and for Selznick has to represent a balance between 'the internal state of the system, the strivings, inhibitions and competences that exist within the organisation' and 'the external expectations that determine what must be sought or achieved if the institution is to survive'. The distinctive 'character' of the institution (or organisation, in terms adopted in this book), and the prevailing mission, will be outcomes of the balance struck between these two functions.

Despite the fact that Selznick was writing at an early point in the emergence of organisation theory, his work has, with a few exceptions, for example Perrow (1972b), frequently been cited but has received little sustained attention. There are probably several reasons for this. One is that Selznick took a highly functionalist approach in a period which was critical of functionalism. A second is that it assumes purposeful organisational leadership in a period when the *Zeitgeist* supported greater participation and a de-powering of leaders. A third is that the notion of institutional survival has not been particularly compelling, especially in education. However, it may be the case that the *Zeitgeist* itself is changing in a way which will encourage a greater attention to Selznick's work. Certainly survival is now a crucial issue for many educational organisations. It is difficult to say whether 'mission' has been a factor on the survival of schools, but when one considers colleges of education, although closures have been to a large extent effected independently of quality and have been somewhat adventitious, there are some instances where a distinctive 'mission' has been the saving of a college.

Although the terms 'mission' and 'character' are very slippery indeed the ideas behind them are worth exploring. It is perhaps easiest to do so in terms of the related functions of leadership. This entails, of course, making the assumption that the head will retain the capacity to exert a strong influence on the direction of the school.

The articulation of a mission

Theories of leadership, even contingency theories of leadership, tend to be mainly concerned with the twin functions of task achievement and social needs satisfaction. Perhaps the reason for this is that the theoretical underpinning of such leadership theory is socio-psychological and thus imposes group or organisational rather than political perspectives. To be sure, leadership theory is ostensibly concerned with policy formulation but in fact has little to say about the leadership skills needs or the practices to be followed in constructing a mission. Moreover, there is some ambivalence in the literature which on the one hand portrays the heroic character of certain leaders and on the other portrays the good organisational leader as someone who appears to take the mission as given and focuses on derived tasks. There is the additional factor that the 1950s and 1960s was a time which saw a burgeoning of management theory but it was also a time when there was a social and political climate which emphasised participation and democratisation and when in consequence the heroic aspect of leadership was relatively low-key—though even in the broader social and political field one had the paradox of an emphasis on the value of participation coupled with the veneration of such leaders as Mao, Castro, Fanon and Debray. Social theories are products of their time and we are perhaps seeing a re-emergence of an older concept of leadership which entails the identification and articulation of a mission. Leadership in this sense is perhaps treated with less suspicion. Hodgkinson (1983) makes the following distinction:

> Administration refers then to the more thinking, qualitative, humane and strategic aspects of the comprehensive executive function, while 'management' refers to the more doing, quantitative, material and tutorial aspects.

When he argues that administration is philosophy in action, in this context, philosophy may be 'in the mode of articulated policy utterances or of inchoate and unaltered values daily translated into action through the devices of the organisation'. As far as the argument of this chapter is concerned, mission can be conveyed either as a clear articulation with the head as the person on the white charger, or can be conveyed much more subtly through a succession of leadership actions which would need careful observation to be distinguished from management as Hodgkinson defines it.

Hodgkinson points four maxims for leadership:

> The leader has four responsibilities. He should:
> 1 know the task
> 2 know the situation
> 3 know his fellowership
> 4 know himself

These obviously have some affinity with Tannenbaum's four 'forces'. Hodgkinson's second maxim can be taken to include the organisational situation, and, of course, Maxim 3 on followership would also imply a knowledge of both the organisation and its environment. Although the contingency theorists, following Tannenbaum and Schmidt, invariably include a knowledge of the environment in lists of management tasks, there is, in fact, relatively little discussion in the literature of the skills required and strategies entailed in the leader transforming the forces in the environment into a mission for the organisation. Hodgkinson gets much closer to this in his conception of administration-as-philosophy. We can explore some of the implications of the construction and presentation of a mission for the head.

An expectation of heads is that they will be alert to the forces in the environment of the school which have potential relevance for its internal activities. These forces can be divided into two clusters. One cluster will contain relevant knowledge of what is happening in the broader educational world. This would largely entail a knowledge of existing and emerging educational policies at national and local levels. This knowledge would be acquired through a reading of policy statements, reports (or, at least, reports of reports), the educational press, and through interaction with other heads, advisers, lecturers, etc. through courses, conferences, in-service days, etc. Underpinning these policies will be a body of educational and curricular theory and associated research on which the well-prepared head could call, to put them in a wider philosophical and empirical context. The second cluster relates to the clientele of the school and would include a knowledge of social background, parental aspirations, community resources, job opportunities, etc.

The head who would create a mission for the school would have the continuous task of selecting from these clusters of knowledge which, as modified by an awareness of forces within the head and within the teachers currently teaching in the school and such other organisational forces as structures and resources, would fashion a set of goals for the school which could be construed as a mission. Different leadership styles entail differences in the degree to which heads construct missions alone or in collaboration with members of staff who would have been encouraged to contribute to the negotiation of a mission on the basis of *their* knowledge of environmental forces and forces within themselves. To the head would fall the task of aticulating and presenting the mission. This would be achieved through verbalisation, through the deliberate deployment of symbols, or through a series of less obtrusive symbolic acts. At this point the task merges into the middle elements of Hodgkinson's model: *politics* and *mobilising*. This involves the securing of staff commitment to the mission. The task then moves to the operationalisation stage and merges with the *managerial* components of the Hodgkinson model. This involves the fulfilment of the two basic dimensions of leadership: task achievement and social needs satisfaction.

Mission and style

The literature on leadership signposts a plethora of styles. Typologies of styles are sometimes derived from wide reading and reflection, sometimes from the close observation of leadership in practice in either small group or organisational settings, and sometimes from statistically generated factors which the investigator then names. Extant typologies sometimes contain few categories, sometimes many. And the styles adduced are sometimes holistic and sometimes related to specific elements in the leadership task. One of the best-known typologies is Weber's distinction between *charismatic, traditional* and *bureaucratic* leadership. A more psychological typology is Zaleznik's (1966) tripartite typology of *proactive, reactive* and *mediative* styles. Reddin (1970) offers a more extended typology including *compromisers, developers, missionaries, autocrats,* etc. However, we can refer again to Hodgkinson's work which offers the following typology of leadership 'archetypes': *careerist, politician, technician* and *poet*.

Any of Hodgkinson's archetypes could conceivably generate a mission. The *careerist* could do so because the self-regarding nature of this type of leader will, in the cause of self-advancement, create a distinctive mission for their organisations. For Hodgkinson this is 'the lowest archetype from the point of view of moral or ethical approbation'. The *politician* could do so through mobilising teachers on the basis of their professional interests in achieving certain educational goals. The politician-leader differs from the careerist because of an interest in the work-group. The probability of the *technician* generating a mission seems unlikely since this style suggests a preoccupation with means rather than ends. But Hodgkinson notes that it is a mistake to treat the technician-leader as value-neutral or value-neutered since the rationality which such a leader expresses can become an end in itself so that once there is a given aim, though it will not be the technician-leader who prescribes this aim, the technician-as-mandarin will endow the rational means to the achievement of this aim with the status of mission. Hodgkinson cites Albert Speer and James Macnamara as examples from the global stage. But, for Hodgkinson, it is the *poet* who is the leader with a mission. Of this archetype he writes:

> According to the theory of archetypes, the true poet would subsume the lower categories. He would therefore be acting on the highest ethical plane and thereby seeking higher states of welfare for his organisation, states not necessarily perceptible to all subordinates since their clear perception would be a function of the leader's greater value consciousness. The poet would transcend the value forms of life associated with the lower archetypes. He has a sense of the unconditioned and the unconditional; an authority intensified by moral force. He may appear as the 'man of principle' or the 'man of conscience' or the 'man of intuition' whose value commitments are such that they cannot be compromised, even if they fly in the face of the sweetest arguments of prudence and calculation.

Hodgkinson is naturally aware of the dangers in this form of leadership, the close line between the guardian and the megalomaniac. He writes:

> Generally, then, for this archetype there can be but one maxim of praxis: beware charisma! The charismatic leader may wish to lead where others cannot or ought not to follow. To beware does not necessarily mean or entail 'Avoid'!: there can be greatness and glory here as well as danger – superlative rewards for superlative risks – but it does enjoin consciousness. Be *aware*! Then choose.

These archetypes are heuristic. They are not rooted in statistical analysis. They are the outcome of a considerable amount of reflection on the nature of leadership. We will not flog them to death here by applying them systematically to case material of educational leaders, though the reader may like to undertake this exercise. However, they are useful points of reference in the subsequent discussion.

The poet articulates and embodies a mission and colleagues respond in an effective way. To be wholly successful this type of leader must have strong elements of the politician in mobilising teachers, and of the technician in ensuring that aims are effectively pursued. The careerist component is less clear. It may be that the poet can be a careerist or that careerism precludes poetry. Of course, this is at the highest level of abstraction and the apotheosis of the headteacher-as-poet will strike many, if not most, readers as a somewhat bizarre notion.

Since there are thousands of heads in this country it would be to fly in the face of reason to assume that many even approximate to the ideal-type of poet. Most are probably making the best of their own qualities and the situations in which they find themselves.

We have our examples of heads as poet-leaders in the independent sector from, say, Arnold to Neill, but in the state schools we have fewer examples for two reasons. One is that it can be assumed that it is harder in a state school for the head to establish a distinctive 'mission', because, despite the relatively high degree of autonomy in the British system, there *are* external constraints and because, although independent schools are, to a degree, 'wild' and must meet the expectations of parents if they are to stay in business, the parents know what they are buying and there is likely to be a greater congruence between the 'mission' of the independent school and the expectations of parents than is the case in the state sector. The other point is that there are fewer accounts of headteachers-as-leaders for state-school heads simply because the schools produce fewer biographies and because it is much more difficult and politically-sensitive to write about a state-school head except in atypical cases. We can only, therefore, hypothesise some patterns for state schools.

Perhaps the basic distinction is between those heads who lead from the front and, if successful, inspire teachers to follow, and those who whilst not lacking a degree of muted charisma, succeed in building a mission through democratic means involving much negotiation. The former kind is more likely to be careerist, to articulate the mission via language and symbol, and to be committed to greater and more radical change. The latter type of head is more likely to convey a mission in a much more subtle way through everyday actions. Within each broad category there will be many variations. Rather than extend a notional typology beyond these two broad models, and leaving the reader to ponder the applicability of Hodgkinson's archetypes, we can end this section with an extract from Elizabeth Richardson's study of Nailsea School (Richardson, 1973) which illustrates the way in which Denys John, the head, sought to create a mission:

> At times – particularly when he had been under pressure from parents or governors about standards of work, of behaviour, of

dress – he would almost lecture the staff on the ways in which he felt they were falling down, though he would be careful to use the pronoun 'we' rather than 'you', thus acknowledging his own share of responsibility for the school's image in the neighbourhood. Sometimes he would offer intellectual leads, in the manner of a seminar leader, through duplicated papers on fundamental topics such as staff participation in policy making, the nature of authority, the theoretical bases of curricular development. Sometimes he would set out proposals, almost in the style of a government report or memorandum, on such problems as the re-organisation of courses, the setting and supervision of homework and the standardisation of assessment procedures. On some occasions he would protect people from their own feelings by avoiding staff discussion of an important event; on others, he would devote a whole meeting to the exploration of attitudes and feelings about such an event. He might introduce a discussion with a careful, detailed explanation of the theme to be considered, or he might wait for others to take the initiative after only the barest of introductions, if necessary holding an uncomfortable silence. In all these situations it seemed that the staff experienced discomfort, either because they felt lumbered with his prepared thoughts and therefore inadequate by comparison, or because they felt helpless, leaderless and so at the mercy of their own uncertainty about what kind of thoughts it would be appropriate to bring forward.

This extract neatly illuminates the way in which a mission can be constructed by the head-as-leader in collaboration with his colleagues. Although typologies such as Hodgkinson's are valuable, there is a need for case studies of the ways in which heads exercise leadership, undertaken by skilful social scientists who also have a high level of literary ability. The process is complex, subtle and heavily reliant on symbolic modes of communication, a theme taken up in Chapter 7.

A suggestive piece of research is that of Hughes (1973) in which, on the basis of empirical evidence, a distinction is made between the head-as-administrator and the head-as-professional. It is through the latter component of the role that leadership is exercised. Hughes' work indicates that the professional head encourages a professional response from colleagues and although the published data does not explicitly demonstrate that professional heads are those who conceptualise a mission in collaboration with colleagues, it is perhaps reasonable to speculate that this is likely to be the case.

The ambivalence of teachers

Teachers are inevitably critical of their headteachers. The range and diversity of the tasks expected of the head are such that they inevitably fall short of teacher's ideals, which themselves may be in conflict. Teacher talk about heads often focuses on the pathos of leadership, the inevitable shortfall between the ideal and the real. These criticisms will be differently expressed, sometimes vitriolically and sometimes more gently in a humorous context. The functions served by this criticism are themselves diverse and beyond the scope of the present discussion. Of particular interest here is the ambivalence of teachers' attitudes towards the mission-building activities of the head and the susceptibility of this activity to criticism and humour.

This ambivalence probably has its roots in the loosely-coupled nature of schools. Teachers value their autonomy and will yield this only with reluctance. This structural autonomy may well be associated with what might be termed a conceptual autonomy, an individualistic commitment to a set of beliefs about teaching which may be largely intuitive (Jackson, 1968) and to a restricted form of professionality (Hoyle, 1974). At the same time, teachers may experience a desire to participate in and identify with a larger enterprise than classroom teaching, the school and its mission. Thus the 'balance between autonomy and control' and the equilibrium point in a loosely-coupled system may have its counterpart in the relationship between a personal classroom mission and a collective school mission.

A school mission identified and constructed by the head may appear as threatening to the individual teacher. A defence against this will be criticism and often ridicule. The head who attempts to articulate a grandiose mission for the school, unless he or she has the charisma to carry along an enthusiastic group of teachers, will inevitably run the danger of being the object of staffroom humour. We have few studies of this staffroom humour but one of the best (Woods, 1979, Chapter 9), whilst not dealing specifically with the issue of mission, illustrates well the vulnerability of the head to teacher humour. The response of the teachers in a Kensington elementary school (Smith and Keith, 1971) to the grandeur, in this case the fading grandeur, of the mission found its expression in humour, the use of 'colouring books', for example, a humorous activity popular at that time.

Yet, although there would seem to be teacher resistance to the articulation of a school mission, as studies by Nias and others have shown, teachers nevertheless respond positively to heads who are providing positive leadership and even a 'coherent philosophy'. This suggests that the head's task of articulating a mission is particularly difficult and sensitive. Teachers will respond to positive leadership, but the pull of autonomy ensures that their response will be guarded and balanced by a self-protecting humour. However, this is an area very much in need of further study.

Missions that fade and missions that fail

In this section we are concerned with two modes in which there can be a decline of a mission which had previously been successfully established. The first mode is the result of managerial entropy. Heads get older and there is the ever-present possibility of a slow winding down. This is not, of course, universal. A. S. Neill sustained his sense of mission until his death at the age of ninety. Of course, there is no hard evidence of the incidence, or indeed the existence, of this phenomenon. There is the evidence of an increase in the rate of early retirement amongst headteachers, but no assumptions can be made about the relationship between this and managerial entropy. Opportunities for early retirement have increased in recent years encouraged by LEAs who wish to create promotion opportunities in a stable state. It is generally held that the greater incidence of early retirement is due to increased stress experienced by heads. But again, it is difficult to relate stress to managerial entropy.

In Britain at least, there is no policy for offsetting the potential run-down of a school mission. There is currently a move on the part of government to subject heads to systematic external evaluation for the first time, but it is not clear so far just how effectiveness will be assessed or whether there will be any attempt to assess the degree to which they have created a mission for the school. Some heads cope with this potential problem by choosing to move to the headship of a different school, not necessarily for promotion or increased salary, but simply to present themselves with a new challenge.

The failure of a mission is quite a different phenomenon and can arise when a head fails to interpret the environment correctly and therefore establishes an inappropriate mission which is doomed to failure, or fails to involve his staff with a sense of mission, or fails to convert the mission into policy or practice. There have been one or two spectacular failures of this kind in education which have received much publicity. However, the educational enterprise is such that spectacular failures are unusual and the shortfall between intention and action does not have the grandeur of disaster. Since, as was argued earlier, organisational pathos is endemic in schools, to some extent all schools are 'failing', and thus a failure of mission is usually a matter of degree.

The reasons for acute or relative failure are usually the result of a misjudgment of one or more sets of forces which impinge on the leadership role. It will be recalled that Hodgkinson's four maxims were that the leader should know the task, the situation, the followers and himself or herself. 'Failure' can result from being unable to fulfil more and more of these maxims. There are examples in the literature of failures of mission due to a head's misjudgment about outside forces. These have sometimes been failures to carry parents along with the mission. Parents are likely to be more conservative than educationists and any mission which involves innovation beyond the experience of most parents should ensure that they become committed to that mission and in those circumstances it is a key task of the leadership of the school to achieve this. In other instances, heads have misjudged the expectations of the local education authority and the mission has foundered through lack of external support or even hostility.

In some other instances, heads have pressed a mission beyond the level of acceptance of the staff and have alternatively found themselves isolated. Michael Duane at Risinghill (Berg, 1968) and Robert Mackenzie at Braehead (Mackenzie, 1970) each had a personal mission which was not accepted by the majority of staff. Terry Ellis at William Tyndale (Auld, 1976) shared a strong commitment to a distinctive mission with some of his colleagues but it was a mission which was violently opposed by others.

A third problem occurs where the head has a mission, succeeds in getting staff committed to it, but it is then found that the task is beyond the professional and organisational means to accomplish. This frequently entails an attempt to undertake a radical restructuring of the organisation, curriculum and pedagogy of the school but the grand design turns to ashes as the practicalities get out of hand and disruption and disillusion follow. This is a case of a head not fully understanding the task which has been set for the school and misjudging the personal capacities required to bring it about.

Two final points can be made about mission and leadership. One is that what appears as a failure of leadership in one school at a particular time may have positive long term consequences for the educational system as a whole. The injunction to know the task, situation, followers and self probably leads to the majority of schools having modest missions and the educational process changing very slowly through disjointed incrementalism. On the other hand, the spectacular failure may be a pathbreaker which others will follow. The second point is that given the turbulence of the environment, the limits to rationality, and the scope for the operation of sheer chance, the failure of a mission may be more due to sheer bad luck than to an inappropriate leadership style.

Conclusion

There is an extensive body of research on organisational leadership including the leadership of schools. This research emphasises the importance of two basic leadership functions – task achievement and the fulfilment of the social needs of colleagues – as essential to effectiveness. The theory also emphasises the contingent nature of leadership and the need to take account of forces outside the organisation. However, two elements are missing from this body of research. One is the recognition of the micropolitical dimension of leadership – the models presented are a little too rational and altruistic. This issue will be considered in the next chapter. The other omission is the somewhat nebulous function of leadership which is the function of identifying, conceptualising, transmitting and gaining acceptance of a mission for the school, an idea or image of where it is heading.

It has been the purpose of this chapter to put this nebulous but nevertheless important aspect of leadership on the agenda. There is a danger that the idea of mission conjures up a discredited view of leadership as a sword-waving man on a charger. Or, because the conceptualisation of a mission is an educational process, there is the opposite danger of seeing such a leader as an ineffective dreamer. Hodgkinson's model of leadership tasks usefully draws attention to the importance of the continuity of the relationship between the policy formulation and implementation aspects of leadership. We need to know much more about how heads formulate policy, and about the direct and subtly indirect and symbolic means whereby it is transmitted.

6 The Micropolitics of Schools

Committee member: You didn't get your own way today, Alec!
Chief Education Officer: You haven't read the minutes yet!

APOCRYPHAL

There is an organisational underworld, the world of micropolitics, which has received only limited attention from theorists and researchers. It finds little place in organisation theory and even less in management theory. It is rarely discussed in any formal context within organisations and it finds virtually no place in the teaching of educational administration. It is almost a taboo subject in 'serious' discussion, yet informally it is a favourite theme of organisational gossip as people talk about 'playing politics', 'hidden agendas', 'organisational mafias', 'Machiavellianism' and so forth. When this aspect of organisational life *is* mooted, for example, on teachers' courses, there is a *frisson* of recognition and although course members have many tales to tell of micropolitical skulduggery, they prefer to tell them in the bar rather than submit them to analysis in the serious context of a course discussion. We know very little about this darker – or lighter – side of organisations. For enlightenment we have to rely on novels, autobiographies, plays and television serials. The Cabinet diaries of Richard Crossman (1975, 1977) and Barbara Castle (1980) reveal what might be termed 'the micropolitics of macropolitics'. The formal political activities of ministers pursued through discussion with civil servants, the preparation of papers for Cabinet, debates in Cabinet and in the House of Commons, speeches to various bodies, etc. can be seen in the context of attempts to mobilise support amongst political colleagues for a particular policy through implicit and explicit bargaining, direct and indirect influence, sweet-talking and even threats. These activities are not wholly confined to policy matters but also to political careers. The television series *Yes, Minister* has become highly popular for its depiction of the ways in which civil servants use their own brand of micropolitics to manipulate their political masters.

Thus the micropolitical aspects of organisations are widely recognised. 'We all know that it goes on' but just what 'it' is remains vague. 'It' also generates a considerable degree of ambivalence as if we did not wish to concede that organisational and administrative processes are anything less than rational.

The domain of micropolitics

Micropolitics can be said to consist of the strategies by which individuals and groups in organisational contexts seek to use their resources of authority and influence to further their interests (Hoyle, 1982). It might be argued that this is simply a definition of management, but, although a clear distinction between management and micropolitics cannot be drawn, it is worthwhile making a rough and ready distinction in order to bring micropolitics into focus. The relationship between the two is that of *figure* and *ground*. They are interactive domains, one does not function without the other and a particular action by an organisational member could equally be described as an managerial or a micropolitical act – perhaps depending on whether or not one approved of it! Thus the two domains are symbiotic but the predominant theoretical focus has been on management as 'figure' and on micropolitics – if at all – as 'ground'. The purpose of this chapter is to explore micropolitics as 'figure'.

Micropolitics is best perceived as a continuum, one end of which it is virtually indistinguishable from conventional management procedures but from which it diverges on a number of dimensions – interests, interest sets, power, strategies and legitimacy – to the point where it constitutes almost a separate organisational world of illegitimate, self-interested manipulation. One can only speculate on the interaction between management and micropolitics. It may well be that micropolitics is shaped by the formal structures and procedures of an organisation. Perhaps these give the organisation a 'dominant' character with micropolitics 'recessive' and limited in scope to the interstices. An image would be the frame of a Georgian window representing the organisational 'structure' and the glass representing the micropolitics. But what is the 'significant' component of a window: the frame or the glass? They are, of course, integral. On the other hand, it could well be that the 'real' life of the organisation is the micropolitical, with the structure either an inert concept ritualistically treated as the determinant of organisational behaviour but in fact having little real influence, or as only given its life by the operation of micropolitics. In practice, the relationship between management and micropolitics will be variable both between kinds of organisation and between organisations of the same kind. It should perhaps be noted that even in 'tight' organisations structure and management are not unaffected by micropolitics. In prisons, for example, although the 'management' has considerable coercive power, the micropolitical influence of the inmates is such that a degree of implicit bargaining occurs (Sykes, 1956).

The essence of micropolitics, and the characteristics which most clearly distinguish this domain from management, are the *strategies* employed. Management, too, involves a variety of procedures which can be termed strategies and which are conterminous with micropolitics at one end of our continuum, but thence a divergence occurs. Bargaining, for example, is both a managerial and micropolitical strategy. In industrial organisations bargaining between management and unions is an integral part of the administrative process. However, bargaining becomes more micropolitical to the degree that it is implicit rather than explicit, outside rather than inside formal structures and procedures, and draws on informal resources of influence. The difficulty is, of course, that whilst formal bargaining is occurring at the management level, there might well be a hidden micropolitical agenda of which all parties are aware and which shapes the formal procedures. As one moves away from this end of the dimension, strategies become more detached from the formal procedures. For example, Pettigrew (1973) indentified four strategies used by a group of programmers to protect their interests: norms which denied the outsider's competence, protective myths, secrecy and control over recruitment and training. Handy (1976) discusses such strategies as the distortion of information, the imposition of rules and procedures, and the control of rewards. It should be noted that those organisational members who have managerial power will also enjoy the greatest access to micropolitical strategies. Thus the head, who has a high degree of authority and can exert a considerable degree of control over organisational activities, will also have at his disposal a wide range of micropolitical strategies.

Strategies are deployed in pursuit of individual or group *interests*. Again some interests are an essential part of the administrative process. These can be referred to as 'professional' interests and centre on commitments to a particular curriculum, syllabus, mode of pupil grouping, teaching method, etc. It would be unusual for the staff of a school to be in total agreement on these matters, but where conflicts occur there are formal means for resolving these. Professional interests become part of the micropolitical process according to the strategies used to further them. Personal interests focus on such issues as status, promotion and working conditions. These interests, too, can be pursued via administrative procedures but are perhaps more likely to be pursued via micropolitical strategies, since they are matters which tend not to be openly discussed. A difficult empirical problem is to distinguish professional from personal interests, since the latter are often presented as the former, as interpretations of the interests of pupils. Thus a demand for increased time for one's subject is presented in terms of its importance to pupils whereas the real interest of the teacher is in personal aggrandisement and empire building. Or a teacher's resistance to a particular innovation may be presented in professional terms as not being in the best educational interests of pupils whereas this may conceal the teacher's personal interest which is to avoid the need to acquire new skills or otherwise upset established routine or even a genuine fear of the unknown (see Marland, 1982).

Interests are pursued by *interest sets*. This term is preferred to *interest groups* since the latter term conveys a greater cohesion and permanence than might be the case. Interest sets will be coterminous with units such as the management team. However, less formal interest sets might emerge. Some of these may have formal membership and administrative status, teacher unions would be an example. Other sets may mobilise on the basis of age: the 'old guard' versus the 'young Turks'. Others may mobilise and on the basis of attitudes to change; Burns (1955) distinguished between *cliques* who were committed to the status quo and *cabals* which were committed to organisational change. Yet other sets may mobilise when specific issues are to the fore. Thus women staff members may constitute an interest set in resisting the expectation that they will act as cooks and washers-up when social events are organised. Still other sets may be based on external friendship groups, based perhaps on common membership of drama societies, choirs, golf clubs, churches, etc. and provide general support for each other on a range of issues. Of course, membership of interest sets will be overlapping and, in matters concerned with school policy, there is the likelihood that interest sets may combine as a coalition, an aspect of micropolitics studied by Selznick (1957) and Bacharach and Lawler (1980) amongst others.

The fourth component of the domain of micropolitics is *power*. In view of the discussion in Chapter 4 there is perhaps little need to elaborate on the relationship between power, authority and influence, save to point out that at the 'management' end of our hypothetical continuum the power will be exercised in the form of authority but as one moves along to the domain of micropolitics, influence will be the dominant mode.

Thus, although it is not possible to draw any hard and fast distinction between administration and micropolitics since they can be virtually coterminous at one end of our hypothesised continuum, micropolitics is more likely to be orientated to *interests* rather than *goals*, *coalitions* rather than *departments*, *influence* rather than *authority*, *strategies* rather than *procedures*.

Some approaches to the study of micropolitics

Micropolitics is not well-established as a field of enquiry. Some of the reasons for this will be obvious from the preceding discussion. There is no clear distinction between the study of organisations, management and micropolitics, and a number of organisational theorists deal with this aspect of organisations. Micropolitics is a proper subject of a variety of disciplines: social psychology, anthropology, sociology, politics and economics, but hitherto no interdisciplinary approach has emerged, nor have the different disciplinary approaches taken much cognisance of each other. A third problem turns on the question of legitimacy. Approaches to micropolitics tend to assume legitimacy and focus on those aspects which are a normal part of management processes, thus neglecting the important non-legitimate aspects of the domain. Finally, insofar as theories have to be tested via empirical studies of some kind, micropolitics will be neglected because the area is so sensitive that data is difficult to obtain — it is clearly tautologous to say that micropolitics is a politically-sensitive area. Nevertheless, in spite of these problems it is perhaps worthwhile to indicate the kinds of approaches which bear on the study of this domain.

Exchange theory has a far broader application in the social sciences than to micropolitics alone, but it is perhaps the most general of social science perspectives which can be applied to the domain. Homans (1961) has developed an exchange theory based on an economic calculus of benefits, which, reduced to a catchphrase, can be expressed as 'You scratch my back, and I'll scratch yours'. Thus A does something for B which has its *costs* in terms of some species of resource. Similarly B does something for A in return which generates costs for B. Both gain from this exchange, that is they both experience *rewards*. When these rewards exceed in some way the costs incurred, the outcome will be *profit*. Homans (1958) erects a microeconomic social theory on this notion of exchange which need not be elaborated here except to note that he makes the functionalist assumption that there is a 'free market' on the exchange of goods and services and that where an exchange relationship is entered into both participants will profit. However, the 'goods' which are traded in these exchanges are unequal and the profits unequal, or one participant may experience a loss. Thus a head has a greater range of resources and can make a teacher – explicitly or implicitly – 'an offer he can't refuse' whereby the 'profit' of the head is greater than that of a teacher. Thibaut and Kelley (1959) developed a socio-psychological approach to exchange at the level of a two-person interaction, developing a schema whereby the continuation of the relationship would occur if the rewards which both parties derived from it exceeded on the basis of what is termed the *comparison level for alternatives*, the likely reward attainable elsewhere for the same degree of effort. As with Homans, Thibaut and Kelley argue that the principles of exchange at this micro-level would apply as one moves through groups and organisations to the macro-level. However, there has been little attempt to extend this work to these levels.

Blau's (1964) theory of exchange in social life differs from that of others in two important ways. One is that it takes more account than other studies of the effects of differential power in social interaction. The other is that it transcends the microsociological level and concerns itself with the *structures* which are operated by the interplay of power and exchange. Blau is not as optimistic as Homans about the attainment of an equilibrium which is equally satisfying to both parties. There are unbalanced exchanges which have their costs as well as their benefits, and behaviour may be as much concerned with minimising unpleasantness as maximising pleasantness. Inevitably, Blau is drawn towards economic models and the use of indifference curves.

Exchange theory has considerable potential for an understanding of micropolitical activities in organisations, but there has so far been relatively little empirical work based on this theory especially in the natural settings of organisational life. This is hardly surprising since such research is fraught with methodological difficulties. Another problem is that it fails to take account of the limits to rationality discussed in Chapter 3, particularly where the material pursuit of self-interest leads to an irrational outcome for all members of the group if each adopts this behaviour (see Skidmore, 1975, Chapter 4 for a discussion of exchange theory).

Exchange is not simply an unproblematic mutual backscratching activity. In many organisations the exchange is formalised and governed by explicit procedures. These are the focus of theories of *bargaining*. Clearly such theories are more applicable to organisational contexts in which management and unions bargain, or where different units within the organisation bargain with each other over, for example, the distribution of resources. Bargaining in schools is less explicit but does occur. There are a number of approaches to bargaining, but since we are here concerned only with illustrating approaches rather than undertaking a critical analysis of the full array, we can take as an example of an approach in this genre the work of Abell (1975). He writes: 'Essentially, then, a bargaining zone comprises a group of individuals (perhaps representing organisations not groups, i.e. other bargaining zones), normatively constrained, but with differing objectives, attempting to arrive at collective decisions through a complex process of influence and bargaining?' A bargaining zone consists of a set of actors, a set of decisions, an assumption that each actor has a clearly defined preferred outcome, an assumption that each actor attaches a clearly defined salience to each decision, i.e. how important he feels it necessary to exert influence, of the outcome. The bargaining zone is 'normatively constrained' because there are broad limitations in what is possible as an outcome. There will also be allocation norms which dictate why the particular set of decisions which fall within the zone do so. Abell depicts the bargaining process as occurring in two phases. The first is the *influence* phase whereby members of the bargaining zone seek to change others' preferred outcomes. Thus A will agree to support B on some issue which is not particularly salient for A in exchange for B supporting A over an issue which is salient to B. This is followed by the *bargaining phase* where actors bargain from their 'influenced' position to a collective decision Bacharach and Lawler (1981) have developed a set of formal propositions related to bargaining which are based on the interplay between power and tactics which, although the examples are based on employer-union bargaining, have their analogies in the less formal contexts of day-to-day exchanges between heads and teachers.

Abell's approach has its most obvious application in the sphere of industrial organisations where bargaining is part of the formal and explicit management process. However, it can be applied to non-industrial contexts, for example the relationship between warders and prisoners (Dawson, 1975) and it clearly has a potential applicability to schools.

The bargaining approach merges with what one might call *formal theories of organisational politics*. Perhaps the systematic theory of this genre is that developed by Bacharach and Lawler (1980). Reference has already been made in Chapter 4 to their approach to power, influence and authority. They summarise their approach to organisational politics as follows:

> An understanding of organisational politics requires an analysis of power, coalitions and bargaining. The power relationship is the context for political action and encompasses the most basic issues underlying organisational politics. As the primary mechanism through which individuals and subgroups acquire, maintain, and use power, coalitions crystallise and bring to the foreground the conflicting interests of organisational subgroups. Through bargaining, distinct coalitions attempt to achieve their political objectives and protect themselves from encroachments by opposing coalitions. Power, coalitions, and bargaining, therefore, constitute the three basic themes in our theoretical treatise on organisational politics.

Their work thus brings together a number of components which have previously been treated separately in the literature: power, structures and interaction. Their middle range theory tends to be more towards the administrative pole of our continuum in that it is more concerned with formal contexts and legitimate bargaining than with the organisational underworld of micropolitics. Their book is concerned with developing a number of hypotheses rather than with converging the political life of organisations *sur le vif*.

Akin to Bacharach and Lawler's approach is the application of *games theory* to organisations. This is a mathematical approach to bargaining and decision-making developed by *inter alia* von Neumann and Morgenstern (1947) and Rapaport (1966), and has recently been explored in relation to the larger political system by Laver (1981). The theorems developed by contributors to this approach are not concerned with flesh and blood actors in real situations – although the behaviour of such actors may be reduced to such theorems – but with the logic of the game. Thus the 'players', the participants in the bargaining process, are assumed to have the capacity to make rational choices and the major concerns of these theories are the logical steps by which actors converge on an optimum solution. Closely linked with formal theories of organisational politics and with games theory is what can be called the *social psychology of influence* which consists of experimental studies and subsequent theories concerning how individuals in face to face contexts seek to influence others.

The next approach to be briefly considered lies on the borders of social psychology and sociology as it is concerned with the study in the rational settings of organisations with the way in which individuals seek to exercise influence by, in Goffman's (1971) terms, 'the presentation of self'. That is how members of an organisation use verbal, physical and spatial strategies in pursuit of their interests. We can term this the *dramaturgical perspective*. The work of Goffman (1969, 1971, 1974) is perhaps the best-known contribution to this general field. In the specifically organisational literature, there is Mangham (1979) whose work brings together a number of perspectives but is perhaps basically underpinned by a symbolic interactionist approach. His key concepts are: *meaning, self, generalised other, socialisation, roles, concepts, interpretations, actions* and *interactions*. He is thus concerned with how organisational members seek to encourage others to share their own definition of the situation in the politics of organisational negotiation and bargaining.

Mangham draws on naturalistic studies of life in organisations. Moving somewhat further towards an organisational sociology which is concerned with obvious micropolitical strategies in organisational settings and generating middle range theories, there is the approach which, in the view of the present writer, is at the heart of the micropolitical domain and which can be called *political studies of organisations*. The major contributors to this field are Crozier (1964, 1975), Pettigrew (1973) and March and Olsen (1976). Crozier has long been interested in how power and influence operate in organisations and has developed the view that organisational processes are best understood by focusing not on formal organisation or on power as a commodity, but on the games which individuals and groups play in order to solve problems, in which power is treated as a bargaining relationship. He argues for a change in paradigm. Wherein the task of the research is to explore how different systems of games can solve the problems which organisations face. He believes that the way forward is to learn more about current games in all forms of organisation and the forms of regulation inherent in these games. This will be best approached by case and comparative studies at the present time with the prospect of formalisation and measurement left until the future. He has written:

> The dominant paradigm revolved around the basic question concerning the structure: how contextual variables determine the basic structural features of an organisation and how these features command the behaviour of the members and the performances of the organisation. The new paradigm emerges first around the idea that the contextual features of the organisation should not be considered as variables determining the structure of the organisation, but as problems to be solved, and second around the idea that structure is not the necessary modal point of the organisation, but that the games with their rational mathematical features as well as their human parameters will be a much more concrete and rich focal point. (Crozier, 1975)

Pettigrew has been concerned with the resources of power which actors bring to the political process in organisations, power such as the control of information (Pettigrew, 1972). There is no distinctive theoretical stance common to the contributors to what we are calling here political studies of organisations. They are essentially concerned with deriving middle range theories from particular case studies — for which Pettigrew, for example, has been criticised by Bacharach and Lawler who believe that formal and testable theories are now possible. But what they have in common is a concern with the space between structures or the relationship between formal structures and micropolitical processes.

Micropolitics in schools

There are very few studies which have focused explicitly on micropolitics in schools. Gronn's analyses of language use in management contexts in schools is one of the few sets of field studies to have been undertaken in natural settings (Gronn, 1983, 1984b). A number of other studies (e.g. Bailey, 1982b) have developed a micropolitical component in the study of other features in the schools. There is a much larger number of studies of school administration from which micropolitical processes can be, if somewhat riskily, inferred. However, on the whole, there is very little and certainly insufficient even to begin to offer any sort of theory or generalisation.

The loosely-coupled characteristic of the schools is likely to be a factor determining the amount of micropolitics. As noted in Chapter 4, the problem for heads is that they have a high degree of authority but the legal sanctions which underpin this authority will only be invoked relatively infrequently. Moreover, teachers have a relatively high degree of autonomy supported by professional norms which inhibit the exercise of legally-based authority of the head. Thus the head's administrative control must depend to a considerable degree on the exercise of latent power and on influence. This would seem to be likely to encourage the head's deployment of micropolitical strategies in the somewhat gaping interstices within the management structure. The present writer has argued elsewhere (Hoyle, 1982) that the movement towards greater teacher participation in school policy, without any change in the head's ultimate responsibility for the internal activities of the school, may have led heads to have greater recourse to micropolitics in an attempt to fulfil this responsibility in the face of staff pressures towards policies which they cannot wholly support. On the teachers' side, micropolitical activity is probably inhibited to the degree that their preoccupations are with their classroom activities rather than school policy. However, insofar as they are involved in policy-making they will have interests – personal, professional and perhaps macropolitical – and may well engage in micropolitics to further these.

For the teacher the stakes involved in micropolitical activity are relatively low compared with those which one might assume to be the case in industrial and commercial organisations. The potential rewards involved, as we will see below, will cluster around the issues of promotion and the quality of the work situation: what is to be taught to whom, when, where and how. One might therefore anticipate teachers' micropolitical activity to be devoted at least as much to protecting work conditions as to furthering educational policies. But it must be noted that although the stakes do not appear to be high, promotion does become a quite salient interest at certain points of many teachers' careers. It should be further noted that although the stakes of protecting one's work satisfaction may not appear to be high, it must be remembered that *relative deprivation* is keenly experienced and likely to motivate teachers to engage in micropolitical activity to redress circumstances which lead to such feelings (Hoyle, 1969a).

As noted in the previous section, the sociological theory which appears to be most relevant to micropolitics is *exchange theory*, although it is worth reporting that the major protagonists see this as a theory which has general applicability to social behaviour and not simply to its more manipulative manifestations. Exchange theory is predicted on the existence of 'goods' and elsewhere the present writer has attempted to classify the kinds of 'good' which might be involved in an exchange between heads and teachers (Hoyle, 1981):

> The head has the following categories of 'goods' available for exchange:
>
> *Material resources* The head has a high degree of control over such resources as books and equipment which he can distribute differentially as part of the exchange process. It is perhaps significant that headteachers tend not to democratise decisions over such allocations.
>
> *Promotion* British headteachers have a greater direct control over

promotion than their equivalent elsewhere. Their freedom to distribute scale-posts within their schools is a powerful resource which may not be brought out openly in a bargaining situation but is no less potent for remaining implicit. Heads also have a crucial role in the promotion of members of a staff to higher statuses in other schools since their references will be a key factor.

Esteem Heads are in a position to increase, or otherwise, the teacher's self-esteem and esteem in the eyes of colleagues through favourable remarks made privately or publicly.

Autonomy Heads are in a position to determine the degree of autonomy enjoyed by teachers by refraining from monitoring their teaching and other activities.

Lax application of rules This resource is somewhat related to autonomy. Heads are in a position to insist on rules being kept to the letter, but as an implicit bargaining ploy they may be willing 'to turn a blind eye' when rules are infringed. They can apply the rules differentially insisting on their observation in the case of teachers they have little regard for, but failing to do so in the case of teachers for whom they have a high regard or whose support they are seeking.

There is an imbalance between the bargaining resources of heads and teachers. The latter have fewer 'goods' to trade and those that they have tend to be symbolic rather than material. Nevertheless, these are important to heads and some examples are:

Esteem The private or public expression of regard for the head as a person and as a professional.

Support The acceptance of the head's aims for the school.

Opinion leadership This is related to support and involves the use of personal influence in the staff group to gain acceptance for the head's goals or authority.

Conformity The acceptance of the rules and procedures laid down by the head. There may be a paradox here whereby the head is lax in the application of rules in those cases where the teachers are most willing to follow them.

Reputation The enhancement of the prestige of the school (and hence of the head) through examination success, sporting success, involvement in community activities, etc.

Thus, although the simple model of managerial authority depicts a head with considerable power over a group of necessarily compliant teachers, the reality is much more complex with implicit bargaining on the basis of different sets of 'goods' shaping the relationship.

The important and difficult question is how the deal involved in an exchange is struck. Some deals will be the subject of explicit bargaining between a head and a group of teachers — perhaps a formal group such as an academic department, perhaps an informal group of teachers who are challenging a proposed policy change. In this instance the theories of bargaining such as those developed by Abell (1975) and others will apply. But although such explicit bargaining activity is a daily occurrence in industrial and commercial organisations, one's hunch is that it occurs less frequently in schools since it is contrary to the professional norms which pervade education. One might hypothesise that the 'deal' is signalled in highly subtle and informal ways, by language, gesture, symbolic action and so forth. It can be approached only through an interpretive sociology or social psychology requiring the immersion of the investigator in the staff culture of the school. Of course, there is no guarantee that an investigator would make a correct interpretation since presumably those who might be involved in an exchange could misread or miss entirely the message.

A hypothetical example of an exchange between a primary school head and a teacher where the message is transmitted and received would be the following:

	Thoughts	*Speech*
Head	This LEA request for a review of the maths curriculum is a nuisance I can't find the time to do it. I wonder if I can con Jim Smith into taking it on? He has aspirations for a Scale III post.	Hello, Jim. How's Mary? Good. No, things aren't too bad but the office is never off my back these days. Look what I've had this morning; a request for a review of the maths syllabus. Maths is more in your line than mine isn't it?
Smith	What's he up to? Is he hinting that I ought to take it on? I don't want extra work, especially discussing a syllabus with the rest of them, but it wouldn't do my promotion chances any harm.	Yes, it is really. That in-service course which you arranged for me to go on was useful. It shouldn't be too hard a job reviewing the maths syllabus in this school.

	Thoughts	*Speech*
	However, I had better not ask for it. That would be too risky.	
Head	He seems to have bitten, so I'll come right out with it.	Yes, I remember that course. Is this review something that you'd be willing to take on? I'd be very grateful.
Smith	I'll take it on, but how do I convey that I have expectations of promotion?	Yes, I don't mind taking it on. It's something which interests me and it will give me a chance to bring some of our colleagues in. And in any case, it will be good experience for me.
Head	It's clear what he's after. How do I acknowledge that I recognise it as a bid for promotion?	Oh good. That's very helpful. Yes, the experience could turn out to be valuable.

This kind of two-person exchange is the simplest form of exchange relationship. There will be many such in the school especially between the head and members of his staff. However, although exchanges may be limited to the interests of only the two people involved, schools are characterised by a network of exchange relationships which constitute a structure perhaps as potent with regard to the organisational character of the school as the formal authority structure. The interests which this system of exchange is designed to further will include personal and professional interests and those where these two types of interest are inseparable in practice. This exchange system will be relatively stable. Patterns will be established which, perhaps to a large extent, depend on the head's leadership style.

For example, let us consider the notion of *investment* (Anderson, 1967): the head can have sufficient 'confidence' in his colleagues to decide that it is a 'low risk' to invest a high degree of responsibility in his staff, or conversely, regard this as a 'high risk' and make little such investment. This 'investment pattern' will be relatively enduring as long as that particular individual remains head and will characterise the basic managerial processes of the school. At another level, the level of professional interests, the pattern may be more volatile as different 'interests' become or cease to be, salient in the school. Because of the characteristics of schools as organisations – especially the characteristic of 'loose-coupling' – and because of the diffuse nature of educational goals, the school is relatively free to focus on particular interests. Some may be salient because of external factors, for example, the publication of a report on multicultural education *Science 5–16*, which generates an interest, or they can emerge as an interest of a group of staff or perhaps even an individual. The pursuit of these professional interests can generate temporary alliances and thus systems of exchange.

Some basic micropolitical strategies

We have no map of the territory of micropolitics. However, the following are some of the more obvious strategies:

Dividing and ruling

This is a political strategy of long ancestry and we may assume that it is an element in the micropolitics of the school. In fact, the school is likely to be particularly prone to this strategy of control on the part of the headteacher because of its structural looseness. There are perhaps two variants of this strategy. One is for the head to avoid full meetings of staff or to call them only as meetings-for-report and to strike separate deals on, say, capitation matters, with individual teachers or departments. Negotiations are easier to handle in a less formal setting than a meeting and this approach avoids comparisons being made between the separate individuals and units until the decision is *fait accompli* and the overall outcome is known, if at all. A challenge would inevitably generate conflict, which teachers generally prefer to avoid, or involve the less favoured individuals or groups appearing to be seeking to take something away from the move favoured. There are some schools, for example, in which the number of available scale-posts and their actual distribution is unknown to the staff as a whole.

The other use of this strategy is to have matters discussed by a full staff meeting with, in the instances where scarce resources are to be disproportionately distributed amongst the parts of the school, the head insisting on taking the role of 'honest broker' and intervening only to resolve disputes between individuals or groups, thus retaining his power to determine events without appearing to be the *fons et origo* of unequal treatment.

Cooptation

This entails the involvement of those whose support the head seeks or whose potential opposition has to be diverted. Cooptation is a well-documented strategy in organisational politics, but the question of how it functions *symbolically* is unclear. One can anticipate here the continuum hypothesised in the next chapter which ranges from the symbolic nature of most social action to distinctive, expressive and conscious symbolisation through speech, actions, artefacts, etc. Cooptation may well cover the entire continuum. At one end is the head's genuine desire to have the voice of some particular individual or group heard in the decision-making process. At the other end would be *tokenism*, the involvement of, say, a young teacher or a woman teacher simply as a symbol designed to quieten opposition. The effectiveness of cooptation will depend upon the interpretations of members of staff which may range from a positive response to the cooptation as an indication that a particular 'voice' is to be heard, through to the position where the cooptation is recognised as symbolic but, as such, a genuine sensitivity to certain 'voices' and a worthy 'symbolic question' through to an interpretation of tokenism as an agreed attempt at manipulation.

Displacement

Teachers sometimes emerge from staff meetings saying: 'What was all that about?' This question suggests that micropolitical activity had been going on but the precise nature of the conflict of interests had not been obvious to those teachers who were neither directly involved nor had interpreted the messages. The 'real' issue had been 'displaced' with the debate centring on a proxy issue. The reason for displacement is clearly to conceal these 'real' interests which might be considered to be professionally unworthy. Thus the strategy is to gain support for the proxy issue. This is clearly one of the strategies available to a headteacher, but it is also available to individual teachers or groups of teachers in their conflicts with each other. The most frequent type of displacement occurs when the 'real' issue of status, identity, working conditions, etc. are displaced by 'professional' issues. Marland (1982) writes:

> This can become institutionalised in the well known 'pastoral/academic dichotomy'. At its worst this divides staff into those who 'care' (often women) and those who 'demand' (often men), and battles are fought ostensibly over the best welfare of pupils but actually over the relative status of a head of department or a head of house. 'Should this pupil be allowed to enter for French O level or not?' is as much about whether the head of department or the head of house should have the last word.

Bennett and Wilkie (1973) describe a conflict between the head of art and the head of science in a Scottish comprehensive school, ostensibly over the professional issue of how wide a choice over their options pupils should have, but in reality the issues in the dispute were about status and power. This was no doubt a correct interpretation of motive made by Bennett and Wilkie as experienced observers of school management. However, the difficulties in interpretation are obvious since in such disputes the balance between the 'personal' and 'professional' motives is perhaps not wholly clear to the protagonists themselves.

Controlling information

How information is acquired, distributed, presented, doctored or withheld is micropolitical. Information may be a 'good' to be exchanged and therefore be an element in exchange theory. But information is also a means of non-negotiable control. It is a powerful weapon in the armoury of headteachers who have access to different kinds of information such as what one might call *policy-related* knowledge: official reports, LEA policy statements, comparative statistical data (e.g. on exam results), *political systems knowledge*: emerging LEA policies, the concerns of LEA inspectors, the views of governors, etc. and *school-related knowledge*: finances, resources, Burnham points totals, etc. This information is amenable to the various 'treatments' suggested above and these constitute a powerful resource for the head. It is unlikely that individual teachers, or sets of teachers, have access to the same amount of information as the head. Nevertheless, a micropolitical strategy on the part of teachers is the deployment of such information as they can acquire. Heads can depend on the fact that by and large teachers will not have the same information resources as themselves, nor will be particularly motivated to acquire it. However, some sets of teachers will have more access than others to certain kinds of information—union representatives, for example, or those teachers who pay particular attention to reports, the educational press, or have some quite adventitious source of information. Those teachers who have, or make it their business to have, access to information are in the stronger micropolitical position. They become informal leaders on the staff unless they have other characteristics which are irritating to their colleagues.

Controlling meetings

Meetings are perhaps less significant political arenas in schools than in other forms of organisation. In primary schools the full staff meeting, held with variable frequency and formality, constitutes the only such arena. In secondary schools the structures, frequency and formality of meetings are more complex. In the educational domain, meetings have been more often studied in universities than in schools, beginning with Cornford's *Microcosmographia Academia* first published in 1908 (Cornford, 1973). The anthropologist, Fred Bailey, has studied committees in various institutions and societies including Western universities (Bailey, 1965, 1973, 1977). His approach is interpretive, as is that of Gronn (1983) who is pioneering detailed studies of committees in schools using as data meeting transcripts which seek to capture, by representing the natural flow of speech with all its power, overlaps and interruptions, the nuances which are so important to an understanding of meaning.

We know little about the functions, especially the micropolitical functions, of meetings in schools, although they certainly have symbolic functions other than those for which they are overtly called, a point to which we can return in the next section. Bailey (1977) makes a distinction between two kinds of committees in universities:

> Some committees offer the opportunity either to shape or to show off an attitude: their proceedings are marked by ceremonial and formality and posturing to an extent which suggests that the exhibition has an intrinsic value and is not being directed towards getting something done. Along with the ceremonial style goes a concern with policy and principle and a tendency to avoid the discussion of persons.
>
> The committees which show the opposite characteristics, being unceremonious, informal, intolerant of expressive posturing, and ready to talk about persons-in-the-round, have the following features: the members think that what they are doing is of practical (not symbolic) importance; the committee is not large; it has a continuing existence; the members are not delegates from outside interests but answer only to their consciences; their proceedings are private and the members are relatively homogeneous in status. Attitude-shaping and expressive behaviour generally are inappropriate, firstly because the members already know one another's attitudes, and secondly because there is a tacit agreement on values, or (which comes to the same thing) an unquestioning acceptance of the book of rules.

It is interesting to speculate on the prevalence of these forms of committee, or the mixture of the two sets of characteristics in schools. The second type of committee identified by Bailey would normally be a committee of a small number of members of staff meeting regularly and coming to share the same values. In schools, the likely contender for this form is the management team. Full staff meetings in large secondary schools are perhaps more likely to adopt the latter form. In primary schools, the full staff meeting would be the only form of committee. One does not have the evidence to say what form staff meetings generally take in primary schools as it is likely to vary according to the head's leadership style. One can hypothesise that the formal committees are, perhaps paradoxically, those in which manipulative micropolitics are most in play. In the smaller 'community' committees, shared assumptions make manipulation both obvious and inappropriate; the mode will be one of exchange, the 'bargain' being implicit but generally understood. In the more 'organisational' meeting conflict will be more explicit but formalised. But because it is more formalised, and because the head cannot guarantee to achieve agreement on an informal 'exchange' basis, he or she is more likely to engage in manipulative micropolitics both before and during the meeting. The following are hypothetical examples of how a head might seek to ensure that a staff meeting arrives at a 'preferred' outcome (Hoyle, 1980):

'Rigging' agendas: The head controls the agenda, thus 'difficult' items can be kept off, worded as a routine piece of business, conflated with less tendentious items or placed low in the order of the agenda.

'Losing' recommendations: We can here envisage a situation in which a head has established a working party to consider a particular issue but does not approve of its eventual recommendations. The strategy would involve referring these recommendations to sets of other committees in the hope that they would go trekking around the consultative system until some group opposed them or until interest waned and the recommendations became inert.

'Nobbling' members: We can again envisage a situation where an item about which the head has strong views *has* made the agenda of a staff meeting. If the head is aware that a group of teachers, perhaps a working party which has been successful in having its recommendations up for consideration, is committed to an opposite viewpoint from that of the head, the latter may make pre-emptive moves to counter this by mobilising support amongst uncommitted teachers. This would be achieved through casual corridor coversations. At the end of an innocuous conversation the 'nobbling' process might occur as follows:

Head: Oh, by the way. Have you seen that the issue of the ten-day timetable is on the agenda for the staff meeting?
Teacher: Yes. I heard that it was coming up.
Head: Apparently Mr Saltro's group is recommending it strongly.
Teacher: So I'd heard.
Head: I think it would lead to problems. Don't you?
Teacher: Well, I hadn't thought about it much.
Head: Don't you think it would cause a lot of unnecessary confusion amongst the pupils?
Teacher: I suppose it would.
Head: So you agree that that is the danger?
Teacher: Now that I think about it, I suppose I do.
Head: Fine. I'm glad there will be someone other than myself pointing this out at the meeting. I take it that you'll make your views known?
Teacher: Well, I'm not one for speaking much at meetings but I

suppose if there's discussion I'll probably say something.
Head: Good.

This conversation might well have had a hidden dimension but this has not been included as an 'alternative dialogue'. We have a case of a teacher without strong views being coopted to the head's position simply out of deference, and in the absence of any strong views. (See Gronn, 1983 for an actual example of a principal 'preparing' the ground for a meeting.)

Invoking outside bodies: The head is the one person on the staff to interact with a wide range of bodies whose activities impinge on the school. This puts the head in a strong position to advance a particular policy, or to stymie one, on the basis of the alleged views of these outside bodies:

'The LEA wouldn't provide the money.'
'The governors seem to want it.'
'The parents seem to be keen on it.'
'I gather the Chief Adviser is strongly against it.'

'Interpreting' consensus: Here one envisages a situation in which there has been a discussion in which relatively few staff members have spoken on some recommendation of the head and these have been roughly divided into pros and cons. At some point the head says: 'Well then, we all seem to be agreed.' The staff are fully aware that no such consensus exists but for a combination of reasons: out of deference, for 'exchange' reasons, or because of the norms which inhibit the call for a vote, the head's interpretation goes unchallenged.

'Massaging' minutes: If the head has chaired the meeting then the responsibility for the minutes is his and he can ensure that they are worded so as to best represent the head's own views.

One of the micropolitical activities of those who run schools and hence chair key committees is to keep matters *off* the agenda. In a well-known paper in the political science field, Bacharach and Baratz (1962) note that politics is as much about what issues are not discussed as those which *are*. This is, of course, largely a matter of style since some heads are much more open than others on what matters are discussed. However, even the most open headteachers may have to use constraining micropolitical tactics to limit what is discussed at a staff meeting in the sheer interests of efficiency. Teachers will bring to staff meetings concerns which are not formally on the agenda. These concerns may be adventitious or they may represent a school-related variation of 'single issue politics'. These might be concerned with specific organisational, usually departmental, interests so that any agenda item is transformed into a concern about its implications for 'the infants' or 'the biologists'. But they may be more general and, one would hypothesise, 'liberal' concerns: financial, multicultural or staff rights—in the latter case perhaps voiced by union representatives. The head is confronted with the alternatives of shutting down discussion, and thus appearing 'illiberal', or of letting the discussion go where it will at the risk of consuming members' time and, more significantly, leading to policies which may be thought to 'distort' the prime tasks of the school. The head must therefore utilise micro-political strategies which will avoid both extremes. In larger organisations such as universities, this can be handled by referring the issue to a subcommittee in the hope that it might disappear or be transformed into an alternative but related policy which can be given general support because it is less 'distorting'. It might be expected that the smaller committee is more likely to ensure a compromise since its 'community' nature might guarantee minimised posturing and a more lenient attitude. However, although this is a possibility for a larger school, it is less of an option for the smaller school, which means that heads must use their micropolitical skills to divert issues, and teachers their own micropolitical skills to keep the issues alive in the immediate arena of the meeting.

School staff meetings can swing towards the 'community' mode of procedure or the 'organisational' mode of procedure, the direction presumably determined by the head's style and the teachers' response. 'Strategic micropolitics' are more likely to occur in the former modes where people use not only the structure but the space within the structure to promote their ends. On the other hand, it is likely to be the case that, although most teachers 'play the game' of an organisational meeting, others may, either through a deliberate deployment of 'conviction micropolitics', or out of a sheer naivety concerning the rules of the 'meeting game', bring a 'community' mode to a formal meeting. Teachers operating within this mode cannot understand why issues which are important to them cannot be discussed openly, authentically and without the hindrance of procedures. Davies (1976) gives an interesting account of a staff meeting at Creighton School which was run on formal lines. The major issue was the representation of sixth formers in the staff meeting. In relation to the distinction between 'community' and 'organisational' modes, this interesting exchange occurs before the meeting when members of staff are discussing the issue with pupils:

> Miss Hart said that even if they got in, they might be disappointed. 'There is not the free-flowing and uninhibited conversation you might imagine.' 'Then what is the point of staff meetings?' asked a fifth former. There were a few cynical smiles from the other members of staff present.

Conclusion

The existence of micropolitics is widely recognised. However, there is a conceptual problem involved in distinguishing between the formal procedures of bargaining and negotiation which are part and parcel of normal management activity and the less formal strategies which interest sets utilise in pursuit of their interests. The study of organisational micropolitics is still very much underdeveloped and currently a number of perspectives are being brought to bear on this aspect of organisational behaviour.

Schools are perhaps particularly prone to micropolitical activity for two main reasons. One is their loosely-coupled characteristic which yield the 'spaces' in which much activity can flourish. The second is the competing forms of legitimacy in decision-making which arise because the formal legitimacy of the head is challenged by alternative professional and democratic forms which are held to be particularly appropriate to schools. This leaves heads with the problem of balancing their responsibility against the expectations of collegiality.

The head has relatively few tangible rewards to induce teachers to work for the school as a collective, the main reward being promotion, or support for promotion, which is perhaps currently of declining value in the context of falling rolls. There is thus a premium on symbolic rewards of various kinds. Exchange theory is perhaps one of the most important theoretical perspectives on micropolitics in schools. However, in schools as well as the larger society, exchange is not necessarily a self-adjusting market and the unequal distribution of power must figure in any analysis of micropolitics. The power-play of the formal bargaining which occurs in industrial organisations is not greatly in evidence in schools and one must look to the manipulative exercise of power through the use of micropolitical strategies in order to understand fully what is happening in schools.

Micropolitics is not a widely researched aspect of schools. It is a very sensitive area in which to undertake research and, moreover, although its existence is widely recognised, there is a reluctance overtly to concede this. One senses it is at odds with many of our assumptions about the values which underpin professionally-staffed organisations. It also raises quite serious minor issues about the training of heads (Glatter, 1982).

The chapter has avoided a discussion of the moral issues involved in the exercise of micropolitics since this is a complex philosophical issue beyond the scope of this book. It would be relatively easy to deplore manipulative micropolitics exercised in pursuit of individual interests, but it is less easy to deplore micropolitics exercised in pursuits of a collective good. This is often recognised and generally tolerated by the manipulated who may admire this: 'The boss has done it again! He's conned us all into a sponsored run!' Bailey (1982) distinguishes between *legitimate* and *non-legitimate* modes of decision-making. Within the legitimate mode he distinguishes the conventions of *democracy*, the *authority of management* and *legitimation through professionalism*. He argues that these different modes of legitimate can be in play at the same time resulting in confusion. He believes that it is within this context of confusion that the more cynical and manipulative micropolitics would arise and lead to a weakening of the belief of teachers in the moral purposes of the school.

7 The School as a Thicket of Symbols

> The world is a forest of symbols
>
> HEGEL *The Phenomenology of Mind*

Symbols are a key component of the cultures of all schools. When Willard Waller so brilliantly discussed 'the separate culture of the school' (Waller, 1932) he was largely concerned with symbols which found their expression through language, ceremonies, rituals, clothing and so forth. Symbols are particularly salient in schools, more so than in perhaps all other forms of organisation with the exception of churches. The reason for this is that schools have expressive tasks and symbols which are the only means whereby abstract values can be conveyed. The instrumental functions of schools are also given symbolic expression since, as far as the pupils are concerned, these instrumental functions are long term and need to be given a more immediate expression through symbols of some kind if they are to be made significant to pupils. There is no doubt that schools are particularly rich in symbols and we are aware of this potency. One could hardly escape recognising this if one were to walk through the buildings and grounds of Eton College. The cloisters are lined with memorials for former pupils killed in two World Wars, sometimes including several sons of the same family and not a few with hereditary titles. Present pupils would be seen wearing dress unique to the school and the knowledgeable observer would be able to detect subtle variations in dress symbolising differences in status. Then there are the playing fields which are much more than the area within which school games are played, not least on account of the observation made by the first Duke of Wellington, since when they have had symbolic significance connoting certain military virtues. And set amongst the other buildings (how inappropriate it would be in this context to say in the middle of 'the campus'!) stands Eton College chapel, so palpably connecting education and Christian belief.

The symbolic dimension of schools is frequently made explicit in disputes about pupil dress and hairstyle which are so gleefully seized upon by the local and national media. Two current manifestations at the time of writing are one of a girl who has been refused entry to an examination because she was wearing red shoes and another of a girl who has been refused entry because her hair was dyed green. The girls' parents insist that they have every right to go to school thus dressed and decorated since these are prevailing fashions and there is no harm in them. On the other hand, the school believes that there *is* harm because these fashions symbolise anti-school values, and hence present a potential threat to social control in the school.

The most theoretically sophisticated approach to the symbolic order of the school is that of Bernstein (1977). King (1969, 1973, 1976, 1981) has been concerned with this dimension in a number of studies including empirical tests of Bernstein's theory. There have been a number of studies of schools and classrooms which have in part been concerned with their symbolics (e.g. Wakeford, 1969; Hargreaves, Hester and Mellor, 1975; Woods and Hammersley, 1977). But as far as the study of the symbolic approach to the organisation and management of schools is concerned, the cupboard is virtually bare. Yet, it is with this dimension of the school that this book is concerned and it will be necessary to draw upon a range of literature to inform what can only be a series of speculations. However, the first task is to explore the basic concept of *symbol*.

The concept of symbol

Perhaps the simplest definition of a symbol is that it represents something other than itself. Modes of symbolic representation are language, gestures, action, dress, spatial relationships and artefacts. However, although this basic definition is serviceable, the concept of symbol is quite complex and the term is used in a number of different ways. We can consider five particular problems.

The first problem is that although an everyday connotation of a symbol would be something which embodies a distinctive expressive meaning such as a flag, the Christian cross, etc. in another view almost any word, act or object can function as a symbol. Thus we have to hypothesise a continuum at one end of which symbols are ubiquitous and at the other end of which they are expressions of condensed meaning.

Let us consider the ubiquity of symbols. An assumption of pervasiveness of symbols is central to the interpretive approach to understanding social life. Actions, gestures and speech symbolise the intentions, wishes and states of mind of an individual. In the process of social interaction other individuals learn to interpret these symbols and hence learn to 'take the role of the other'. Through the reciprocal interplay of symbols, common understandings emerge and become established as relatively stable sets of meanings. These meanings may be universal and shared by the human race or they may be limited to a relatively small social group. The explorers who opened up Africa were able by means of gesture to symbolise their needs – for food, shelter, transport, etc. – and their willingness to barter. This was possible because humans share the same biological needs and because certain social institutions are near-universal.

Symbols are not only the means whereby established meanings are communicated but are central to the process of *constructing* meaning. Mead (1934) wrote: 'Symbolisation constitutes objects not constituted before, objects which would not exist except for the context of the social relationship wherein symbolisation occurs.' Mead treated language as a symbol system and as such as having a crucial role in the creation of meaning. He continues: 'Language does not simply symbolise a situation or object which is already there in advance, it makes possible the existence or appearance of the situation or object because it is part of the mechanism whereby the situation or object is created.'

In the symbolic interactionist view of Mead and others, our daily lives are spent responding to symbols which, in cueing behaviour, are largely taken for granted and have no special significance. If one moves along our hypothesised continuum these symbols become fewer but have a higher degree of salience because they mark out what is of particular significance for a group, what it endows with special value.

This continuum can perhaps be expressed in another way by brief reference to the theory of signs. A *denotative* sign simply *stands for* an object. A denotative sign is typically a word, thus the word 'school' stands for the group of buildings, membership and activities of an organisation established for the purpose of educating children. A *connotative* sign goes beyond denotation and conveys a set of feelings, associations and suggestions, and is responded to more affectively by those groups for which it has connotative significance. In the sentence: 'He is training to be a teacher', the term 'teacher' is a denonative sign standing simply for membership of an occupation. But in the headline: 'Teacher accused of theft' the term 'teacher' connotes a wider set of associations concerned with probity, responsibility, etc. Jaeger and Selznick (1964) suggest that it is this connotative nature of signs which enables them to function as symbols, but in their view, connotative signs are not in themselves symbols. As they put it: 'A sign becomes a symbol when the sign is responded to directly as a carrier of connotative meaning'. Thus a sign is instrumental in pointing to something other; a symbol is expressive in that it evokes a direct response. Thus true symbols are emblems, flags, ceremonies and so forth. The buildings of Eton College constitute symbols because they not only connote certain values but are responded to directly as such. They are a palpable expression, for some, of the values of scholarship, gentlemanliness, etc. However, the distinction between what is only a connotative sign and what is a symbol is difficult to determine. It depends on context, the shared understandings of those responding to it, and so forth.

We can stay with the theory of signs to explore briefly the status of language as symbol. There is a view that all language is symbolic. We have already referred to the symbolic role of language within the interactionist perspective and cited G. H. Mead on this topic. But also within the theory of signs there is the position that words are symbols which correspond to objects, feelings, ideas, etc. However, we are here concerned with the ways in which words function as symbols as Jaeger and Selznick use the term. If we take the word *school* we can construct a hypothesised continuum of symbolic use with four points. One point is where 'school' simply denotes a particular kind of organisation. But 'school' can also be a connotative sign generating a wider set of overtones. In the sentence: 'My son loves school' the word connotes a set of activities and relationships which the boy enjoys, yet this is probably not a word-as-symbol in Jaeger and Selznick's terms. Moving further along the hypothesised continuum we can cite the phrase 'letting the school down' as containing the word which verges on the symbolic, a concept which is responded to directly. At the far end of the continuum one can cite the Old Boys' dinner of an independent school where a toast is proposed to 'the School'.

A second problem arises when we consider the *function* of symbols. It stems from the fact that the meaning of a symbol is socially constructed. One cannot know the meaning of a symbol without reference to a group which is responding to it (or failing to respond to it). Ultimately this is an empirical question. Responses to a potential symbol must be ascertained by the standard modes of collecting data on issues such as these. But we can briefly elaborate some theoretical possibilities here. In the sense in which we are using symbol – as a word, object or action which has a relatively high level of significance for particular social groups – what is symbolic for one group may have no symbolic significance for another. The cross has symbolic significance for Christians and the crescent for Moslems, but not vice versa. A statue of the Virgin in a Roman Catholic school will have symbolic significance for a Catholic but not for a non-Catholic visitor. However, here we have another problem. A non-Catholic visitor will respond to the statue as a symbol *cognitively* without necessarily responding to it *affectively*.

A third problem which arises is the fact that a symbol may simultaneously stand for quite different values and beliefs. The buildings, dress, etc. of Eton symbolise for many people scholarship, gentlemanly values, patriotism and the beliefs of the established church. But for others they may symbolise elitism, capitalism, militarism and patriarchy. There is no denying the symbolic significance of the dress and the buildings, but the significance lies in the eye of the observer. Not only visitors but also pupils, to judge by the memoirs of old boys, respond differently to these symbols. This variation in meaning is only one of the difficulties attaching to the study of symbols with which this chapter will be concerned.

A fourth problem is that a symbol can represent the *reality* of values, power, status, etc. or can be a *substitute* for reality. In everyday usage, the expression: 'it is only a symbolic gesture' means that what is occurring is designed to displace reality. Thus a dissident group may not 'really' be consulted by those in power, the 'consultation' is purely symbolic. Similarly a new title bestowed on a member of staff may not indicate any 'real' change in status or power but is a symbolic act perhaps designed to allay disappointment that the person was passed over for the 'real' promotion.

A fifth problem arises because of the possible disjunction between intention and interpretation. At one extreme a head might deliberately seek to utilise symbolic means to generate support amongst the staff of the school, but this intention remains unfulfilled because the teachers fail to recognise and hence respond to the symbol. Elizabeth Richardon (1973) provides an example of this. At Nailsea School the head and senior staff agreed a set of names for the new houses which had been established – Pegasus, Dolphin, Pelican, Heron – which were intended to symbolise certain virtues. But this was lost on the pupils and on most of the staff. At the other extreme, the teachers may interpret as having symbolic significance some chance remark by the head, a notice which has been circulated, or an obscure staffroom conversation between the head and a teacher when there has been no intention thereby to convey any message of symbolic significance.

No particular connotation of the concept of symbol is adopted in this chapter and the discussion will range along the continuum from the general to the special. However, though schools are particularly rich in symbolisation, the focus will be on the role of symbol in the management process.

The head as meaning-maker

A number of organisational theorists have noted the importance of the symbolic dimension of leadership. Indeed it has been held by some writers that leadership is a largely symbolic activity. Even in the industrial sphere Weick (1976) noted that the manager was 'more of an evangelist than an accountant' and held that managerial work could be viewed as managing myths, symbols and images. Pondy (1978) argued that one of the major tasks of managers was 'to give others a sense of understanding of what they are doing and especially to articulate it so they can communicate about the meaning of their behaviour'. (See also Smircich and Morgan, 1982.) If organisational theorists insist on the importance of symbolic action for industrial management, how much more significant is it for the educational manager, the head? Few heads will avoid constructing an image of the school. This will differ in the degree to which this is a deliberate and charismatic task. Some heads, the Dr Arnolds *de nos jours*, will self-consciously seek to construct a great mission for the school. Others will convey their idea of the school less dramatically and construct a meaning from the basic materials of symbol-making: words, actions, artefacts and settings. Out of these materials they construct presentations, create myths and devise stories.

Language is central to this process. One would need detailed studies of heads' language use in context to understand how a particular meaning was constructed. However, there is little doubt that some key terms can be particularly salient. In Kensington School, for example, the key term was 'flexible'. This became a summary term which acted as a symbol representing the distinctive characteristic of school organisation and curriculum (Smith and Keith, 1971). Another word which is often endowed with symbolic significance is 'community'. This is used in at least two ways. One is as a broad expressive term intended to represent the school to itself as having *Gemeinschaft* qualities: 'this school is a community' or 'a caring community'. But the term can be used more instrumentally in the case of schools which are 'community schools'. The 'community' of a community school can be more realistically conceptualised as a set of associations and its role symbolised in a more instrumental way. This approach is implicit in the conceptualisation of the Sidney Stringer Community School and College by Geoffrey Holroyde, its first head, who wrote as follows in the Staff Manual:

> It may be that we can pick out groups of people in (the) Community, for example:
> – Young people of compulsory school age
> – The parents of those young people
> – Adults and young people over school leaving age
> – Members of recognised and established groups
> – Professional teachers, community workers, social workers, health visitors, politicians and other agents.
> Such groups may have little in common, and the college does not attempt to force them into artificial association with each other. There is no 'one' community, but an amalgam of many formal and informal groups working and playing alongside each other.
> (Quoted in McHugh, 1976)

The symbolic significance of the term *management* is interesting. In many ways it symbolises a very different mode of integration from community, although in some instances – as in the Sidney Stringer Staff Manual referred to above – a particular model of management is combined with a particular conception of community. However, broadly speaking whereas *community* symbolises the *Gemeinschaft* quality of the school, *management* symbolises its *Gesellschaft* or instrumental character. The use of the term *management* to apply to the coordination of the activities of schools has been in general use for not much more than twenty years. *Management* symbolises a rationalistic approach to the coordination of schools. Notwithstanding the fact that the majority of schools are primary schools and structurally relatively simple organisations, there has been a widespread adoption of the term for the running of schools. In secondary schools it is now common for heads to establish a *management team* and to have a *middle management* level in the school. Some have adopted the approach of *management by objectives*. We are not of course concerned here with the management structure and processes, but with the symbolic role of the word 'management'. One function may well be to induce teachers whose main interest is in teaching and not in administration to accept managerial roles. By adopting what is essentially an industrial term it is perhaps hoped to endow these roles with status. A second function may well be to convey to the world in general the complexity of running a school and that the skills required are akin to those required to run an industrial or commercial enterprise. A third possible function is the encouragement of the self-image of the teachers as pursuing a 'masculine' task. Perhaps this self-image appeals not only to men but to women who seek management roles in schools – and there are far women fewer than men – who see the term 'management' as symbolic of their capacity to fill masculine roles (whilst, perhaps, remaining very feminine).

These are only some of the more obvious words having a widespread symbolic significance. However, language is undoubtedly much more subtly symbolic than this, and in all schools words which would not normally be held to be heavily symbolic become so because their symbolic significance is endowed with a context of common understandings. Indeed one organisational theorist has suggested that a profitable way to conceptualise organisations is as *speech communities*. However, organisational theory, and even less so organisational research, has not hitherto attended to this issue. There are, as readers will recognise, enormous conceptual and methodological problems and interpretive perspectives in sociology and social psychology for ways of understanding the symbolic significance of language in organisations. In education there is a growing body of studies dealing with language in classrooms from which the student of the school as an organisation can draw insights, and a pioneering approach to the study of language-in-use in the context of educational management is that of Gronn (1983).

Much can be learnt about the role of the head in using symbols to create a meaning for the school from the material relating to Countesthorpe College and the role of Tim McMullen, the first Warden, particularly the case material prepared for the Open University course E 203 (Prescott, 1976). The cover sheet for this material shows Tim McMullen photographed against the background of the school buildings. These buildings themselves have symbolic significance. As the photographs and the plans show, the school's open design with coffee bars and comfortable chairs for pupils as well as staff symbolise an egalitarian relationship and the treatment of pupils as responsible people. McMullen, in the cover picture and elsewhere in the material, is invariably dressed in a short-sleeved, open-necked shirt symbolising informality and direct, purposeful involvement in the school, contrasting with the stereotype of the dark-suited, formal head. Photographs of the staff show the same informality of dress and generally unbuttoned style as they sit with each other and with pupils on chairs and on the floor. (Though it should be noted that these photographs themselves have presumably been selected because they 'symbolise' the organisational culture of Countesthorpe.) The radical nature of the curriculum was symbolised by the invention of a new nomenclature for different components, e.g. 'CW' (Creative and Expressive Words, Music and Drama), Two D and Three D (Creative and Expressive Arts and Crafts) and Ig (The study of the individual and the group). The full staff meeting was termed 'the Moot' to symbolise its plenary and participative nature. These and other symbolisations created the 'idea' of a highly progressive state secondary school. It is difficult to say how far this 'idea of a school' was adopted by the staff. From the literature about the school it would appear that many did so and the symbols represented their aspirations in joining the school staff, whilst others did not. But the symbols seem not to have been particularly effective in conveying the 'idea of the school' to parents and the community. It would seem that for many the symbolic representations helped to convince them that the school was not what they wanted for their children.

In interesting contrast is the symbolic presentation of the idea of a school is reported in a case study of a comprehensive school pseudonymously called 'Hillford' (Gilbert, 1979). Check lists and external ratings confirmed this to be a highly innovative school yet the head appeared to be concerned to present the school symbolically as a relatively conservative organisation. What Gilbert demonstrated was that two sets of symbols were in play, one set for the staff and one for parents, and that for the head himself this 'Janus-faced' representation of symbols was intentional. He was educationally-conservative at one level and emphasised the importance of uniform, high standards of behaviour, firm discipline, examination success and other goals which would appeal to the largely middle class parents. He was himself tall, had an erect, military bearing, was formally-dressed and spoke with charismatic authority. He was greatly trusted by the parents. He symbolised the same values internally within the school vis-à-vis the pupils but also fostered a high degree of innovation by, in essence, encouraging staff to generate curriculum change and, in fact, deliberately appointing innovative teachers to posts vacated by those teachers (an impressively high proportion) who were promoted. The symbols of traditional schooling remained, and innovations in the curriculum were not to threaten good examination results – the external symbol of a successful school – but innovation flourished in an environment protected by a symbolic conservatism.

The organisational myth

This organisational myth is the extreme case of the making of meaning. The myth can be fostered by the head or by the teachers themselves – as when they sustain the 'Rebecca myth', the image of a golden age which preceded the arrival of the present head. A myth is essentially a story which the organisation wishes to tell about itself and continually tell *to* itself in order to sustain a sense of identity. The myth, like all stories, will be exaggerated, heightened for effect. Others have used the term *organisational saga* (Clark, 1972) and *rhetorical community* (Bormann, 1983) for the same phenomenon. One should also add that it is possible for two sets of participants, opposed in their interests, to construct different and competing myths.

Perhaps the most sustained study of the creation of an organisational myth is Smith and Keith's (1971) study of Kensington. However, they do not explicitly use the notion of myth. Their guiding metaphor is, in part, that of a *crusade* and they draw upon Hoffer's (1951) work on 'the true believer' and Klapp's (1969) work on crusades. They note the ways in which the true belief was built up and sustained. One of these was the use of 'the image of evil', that is of wrongs to be righted. One of these 'wrongs' was conventional elementary school education. This was sustained by the use of cult jargon, so that conventional elementary education was labelled as 'four by two' education, i.e. the four walls of the school and the two covers of a textbook. As in the case of Countesthorpe cited above, the faith was supported by symbolic use of language. As Smith and Keith point out, nothing at Kensington was called by a usual name. Teachers were 'academic counsellors' or 'resource specialists', classrooms were 'laboratory suites' and the library was the 'perception core'.

Murray (1983) undertook a study of two primary schools in close proximity to each other in a town in Northern Ireland, one Protestant and the other Roman Catholic. This sensitive study, in the two meanings of this term, showed how each school had its own myth and that each was to some extent sustained by the myth which was projected on to it by its neighbour. Murray was able to show not only the power of these sustaining myths, but also how the projections were not always in accordance with the facts. As one might expect in these circumstances, the myths were fed by religious belief and by nationalist or republican sentiment, but it was interesting that the myths also embrace aspects of school management, curriculum development, staff development and academic achievement.

Mobilising support and quieting opposition

These are the functions of symbolisation identified by Pfeffer (1981a). Bearing in mind the distinction made above between *intention* and *interpretation* these functions are intentional, but the interpretation which others will place on these symbolic

THE SCHOOL AS A THICKET OF SYMBOLS 161

purposes may be congruent with the intention, if the head is skilful in using symbolisation for this purpose, or maybe ineffective and have unintended negative consequences. We can explore some of these issues by hypothesising some examples of management strategies which may have deliberate symbolic interest or can be interpreted as having such.

Association

This very broad term is used here to cover various patterns of interaction between heads and their teacher colleagues. Perhaps one can illustrate the symbolic significance of interaction by citing the no doubt apocryphal story of the man who asked John F. Rockefeller for a hundred thousand dollar loan. Rockefeller replied that he would not make him the loan but what he would do would be to walk across the floor of the New York Stock Exchange with his arm round the man's shoulder. The effectiveness of this symbolic gesture would obviously depend upon interpretation. Headteachers will have differential associations with colleagues. Some, such as those with members of their management team, will be school-related, others may well be the results of relationships outside the school.

Obviously, any distinctive relationships will be capable of symbolic interpretation — the head favouring a particular individual or group, or such individuals or groups seen as seeking favour. The head may also seek intentionally to endow relationships with symbolic significance or part of a strategy of mobilising support and quieting opposition. For the staff as a whole this may take the ritual form of an annual garden party hosted by the head. But within the school the associations can take many forms from informal conversations through to semiformal consultations.

Space

The symbolic properties of spatial relationships are widely recognised. Space, which is interpreted as territory, often has symbolic significance of an intensity which sometimes astonishes the outsider, and sometimes the insider. The present writer recently had to engage in the reallocation of rooms within the main departmental building. Of course, one was fully aware of the significance for status of room-size and location, but it so happened that no-one who was to be involved would need to move into a smaller, or ostensibly, less prestigious room. In fact, most of those moving would end up in larger rooms. However, it emerged that rooms had a symbolic status far beyond their more obvious status implications of a kind which the present writer was unable to fathom even after discussions of the issue with the people involved. Certainly the view from the window was important, as was the relationship to the sun, although some wanted sun-filled rooms whilst others did not. But underlying the preferences was a social geography, some of the implications of which could be interpreted, but others defied any obvious explanation. Moreover, the writer became conscious of the different interpretations of symbolic significance which were attached to his proposals, some of which bore no relationship whatsoever to his intention, some of which did bear relationship to his intention and some which brought to a level of consciousness intentions *which he had not been fully conscious of holding*.

No doubt the allocation of rooms in schools has intended and unintended symbolic significance. The head may choose to allocate rooms on the basis of symbolic significance for status, power and control, but only an intimate knowledge of the school would allow an understanding of both intention and effect. If a primary school head allocates the classroom nearest his or her own room to a particular teacher, this may be a positive symbol in that it indicates the head's preference for having the teacher nearby for consultation or informal interaction or a negative symbol in that it indicates the head's wish to maintain close supervision over the teacher. Similarly, the allocation of a prefab across the playground may symbolise the head's confidence that the teacher concerned does not need close supervision, or a wish to isolate the teacher from the main school and thus from observation by visitors. Goffman, whose work is concerned with the transmission of symbolic meaning in organisational groups and face-to-face contexts and should be read by anyone interested in this field, gives numerous instances of the acceptable face of an institution which is kept at the 'front' and readily observed and the unacceptable face which is kept in the 'rear' and away from the observation of visitors (Goffman, 1969, 1971, 1974).

The symbolic utilisation of space in face-to-face contexts is well known and again discussed by Goffman. The use of space in staffrooms by headteachers, should they be in the habit of using staffrooms – itself symbolic – is an action to which it is possible for teachers to attach different interpretations, for example the head-as-friendly-colleague or the head-as-snooper, although there are few detailed ethnographic studies of this aspect.

Heads may manipulate space in their offices in symbolically-significant ways. For example, some heads have, apart from an office chair behind the desk and straightbacked chairs in front of it, two or more easy chairs arranged around a low table and/or straightbacked chairs around a 'conference' table. The head's use of this space and furniture will symbolise intent, which may be 'telling' (sitting behind the desk with the teacher standing, or sitting on a straightbacked chair), 'discussing' (sitting round the conference table with colleagues) or 'asking' (sitting in an easy chair with colleague, or colleagues, sitting in the others).

Time

The adage has it that 'time is money'. Time is also an indication of value status and power. Many of the present writer's higher degree students write an assignment which explores the micropolitics of a critical incident in their own organisation. Time and again the critical incident discussed is a proposed change in the allocation of time on the timetable for some subject or activity. Timetable allocation is taken as an indicator of the status of a subject and hence of those who teach it. Any reduction will therefore be hotly contested (Bailey, 1982b).

Meetings

Ostensibly formal meetings are called to transact school business either in a full staff meeting or in various subcommittees and working parties. But meetings are rich in symbolic significance both *as* meetings and in the forms they take. Meetings with the same format may have quite different functions in relation to the head's attempt to gain support. The function for the head may include reporting, instructing, remonstrating, advising, mobilising, threatening, socialising or some combination of these and other functions. Yet whatever the function as far as the head is concerned, the formalities will be the same. The teachers have the task of interpreting the purposes of the meeting and they may endow a meeting with functions which are significant to them. These are the 'hidden agendas' of micropolitics and are symbolised in various ways including the setting of the meeting, formal and informal seating patterns, the degree and nature of 'meeting etiquette', etc. Swidler (1979) reports the conscious use of school meetings involving both staff and students in an American free school as a medium for sustaining a collective identity:

> Although time-consuming meetings may be necessary to preserve the values of direct democracy and to assure broad participation in decisions, Group High's meetings were drawn out far beyond the time required for actual decision-making. Since meetings served an expressive, solidarity-building function, teachers took every opportunity to prolong discussion, suggest new complications, and turn practical decisions into occasions for exploring basic values, goals and commitments.

Roles

It is in the micropolitical contexts of meetings that the dramaturgical aspect of organisations is most salient, particularly in the larger, formal meeting in which 'performance' replaces the easier, more intimate, perhaps more 'authentic', smaller meetings which engage individuals as persons rather than roles. The concept of 'role' is quite complex, but we can make a rough distinction between the formal roles of deputy-head, head of department, etc. and the more dramaturgical roles. The distinction is between 'playing roles' and 'playing at roles', although the latter obviously is not wholly akin to an actor playing a part since these roles are more authentically a representation of attitudes and beliefs. Bailey (1977) writes: 'The metaphor of the drama suggested in the words "mask" and "character" should not be misunderstood. It is not that *all* the world is a stage, but only that *in the world of politics* no one ever wins without having at least some capacity to be a "player" — to present in a bold, simple, indeed, caricatured fashion some side of himself or his policies that will captivate his supporters and intimidate his rivals.' Bailey discusses a number of masks including *Reason*, 'the technician of the intellect', *Buck* who believes that 'anyone will do anything if the price is right', *Sermon*, 'the guardian of our eternal verities', *Stroke* who believes in a world where people are made orderly by being 'stroked' into place, *Saint* who is 'prestuffed with all the goodwill of the world', *Baron* 'who in every situation sees but two possibilities: to screw or be screwed', and finally, *Formula*, who 'believes that solutions already exist in the regulations and need only be applied to particular situations'.

This is only one particular set of masks. Marland, citing Richardson's (1973) observation that members of a school management group can play both instrumental and symbolic roles, writes:

> I have seen discussions on one matter turned by participants who 'stand for' one part of the staff's feelings into quite a different matter. The symbolic roles can be seen as facets of each of us, so that one teacher 'becomes' 'overwork', another 'idealism', another 'the cry for more resources', and yet another 'bloody-minded resistance'. On these occasions one is not listening to a functional role-holder, 'the head of science', but a symbolic speaker for perhaps unspoken feelings using this moment as a suitable opportunity.

Documentation

The documentation which an organisation produces about itself can have symbolic significance. In fact, schools tend not to produce much documentation about themselves, but what *is* published by way of handbooks and guidelines for parents can be rich in symbolic meaning. Richardson (1973) writes most interestingly about the staff lists which appeared over a three-year period in the Nailsea Journal, a compendium of information about the school which went to governors, parents and others. The names of the head, deputy and senior mistress were printed at the top of the staff list. These were followed by an alphabetical list of all other staff members followed in each case by the person's job designation. Changes occurred in these designations from year to year which were symbolically highly significant. They revealed ambiguities about individual statuses and functions and the sensitivities thereby involved, but also revealed ambiguities about the very nature of the school structure itself. Richardson rhetorically asks: 'Was the compilation of the journal just "a straight administrative job"; a chore even? Or was it something more?' It *was* something more, and one would contend that such a task, unless it involves simply listing names alphabetically, can never be simple. In fact,

Richardson hypothesises that the changes which occurred revealed the feelings of ambiguity about his own role by the teacher who compiled the list.

Symbols as surrogates

As noted earlier, a symbol can *represent* something which is 'real' in the sense that it has a substantial factual basis or acts as a *surrogate* for reality. Sometimes this is not recognised by those manipulated by symbols who may continue to believe that they have achieved the substance. Often, however, there will be a mutual recognition by the parties concerned that the substance has not been evoked but they are nevertheless content to sustain the fiction that it has if there has been some symbolisation of the substance.

Perhaps one of the aspects of management in which this is most relevant relates to innovation. This is the phenomenon of 'innovation without change'. It is true that changes *do* occur: schools are restructured, new curricula agreed, new teaching strategies formally adopted and so forth, but in reality the system carries on as formerly.

One symbolic action is to change the words used to refer to a particular piece of organisational activity whilst leaving the activity untouched. Although the example comes from teacher education rather than from schooling, one can illustrate the point by noting that courses in teacher education are currently expected to contain a substantial component of work on multicultural education, but whilst some organisations have explicitly and actively included new components on this topic, others argue that they have adopted a 'permeation model' whereby multicultural education occurs in many different aspects of the course. In these instances actual changes *may* have occurred in the course as a whole including more work on multicultural education, but the 'permeation model' may simply be a way of re-labelling what is already happening and therefore the course remains unchanged. Another form of re-labelling as a symbolisation of change is in the re-designation of jobs and changes in titles attaching to roles.

Although symbolisation can be a substitute for change, Peters (1978) has argued that change can actually be *achieved* through symbolic administrative actions. He cites the following as examples of symbolic strategies leading to change:

1. Spending an increased amount of time on an activity in order to emphasise its importance.
2. Changing the settings for particular activities in order to alert participants to the fact that something of consequence is occurring.
3. Exchanging status for substance which entails obtaining the support of a relatively uninvolved group for a particular change by ensuring that the group experiences symbolic reward.
4. Interpreting history in such a way as to endow the proposed solution to a problem with a legitimation based on the organisation's past.
5. Coining a simple phrase to express a dominant value and hence providing an explanation in a rationalisation of a particular activity.

Although Peters lists symbolic actions which can generate change, it will be clear that the actions so defined are not wholly dissimilar from those which are a substitute for genuine change. Only a careful study of the context and the effects or otherwise of this action would determine whether or not actual change ensues.

Conclusion

Although the concept of symbol itself is unclear, there is little doubt about the significance of the symbolic dimension of the school. Whilst management theory, and much organisation theory, focuses on structures and management processes, these may well only be the surface features of the school. The 'reality' of the organisation may inhere much more in the ways in which members utilise and respond to symbols. The significance of the symbolic domain of organisations has recently emerged as an interest amongst a number of organisation theorists. (See the issue of *Administrative Science Quarterly*, Fall 1983.) Because of the diffuse nature of its goals, and because of its expressive functions, the symbolic order of a school is important to its understanding and this has been recognised particularly by curriculum theorists and classroom interactionists. It is, as yet, an underdeveloped aspect of the study of school management, though there is a case for believing that management processes in the school are more important for their symbolic than their ostensibly more rationalistic character. The making of meaning is a particularly important task of the head.

Although this chapter has been largely concerned with the symbolic action of headteachers, it needs to be emphasised that teachers themselves have access to a wide range of symbolic resources for signifying support or opposition.

8 Conclusion

The school is a loosely-coupled system. Its components are centrifugal. The task of the head is centripetal. Herein lies the central characteristic of the school as an organisation. The core professional task of the teacher is the transmission of knowledge, skills and values. Despite the flurries of interest in team-teaching which occur from time to time in some schools, the professional task of the teacher is essentially an isolated one as far as other teachers are concerned, although in this respect no different from other forms of professional practice. The teacher's identity is with a class of children in primary schools and in secondary schools with a subject and a larger number of classes. The teacher is unlikely to identify with the school unless there are strong motivational factors involved. In the secondary school, the specialist teacher can identify fairly easily with his or her subject department because this is identity-sustaining. But whilst a teacher may identify with the school as a whole at a symbolic level, this is rather different from identifying more specifically with the school as an organisation.

Yet schools could not function on the basis of individual enterprise. Some collective purpose and some means of securing at least some degree of commitment are needed. There are two basic modes of securing this. One is through a pattern of coordination which is essentially top-to-bottom and involves some form of management structure. The other is through a pattern of integration which is bottom-to-top whereby structures emerge from the collaborative practice of teachers. The most common mode is coordination. In the 1960s and later there were genuine attempts in some schools to achieve a collectivity of purpose through the mode of integration. However, for reasons which may be more socio-political than purely organisational, this approach did not flourish after the early 1970s. It would appear that the extreme forms of either model are uncongenial to teachers, and as many commentators have noted, the loose-coupling pattern prevails though it varies from school to school and over time. It essentially provides a structure within which teachers enjoy a degree of freedom in the exercise of professional practice, and an authority pattern which represents a balance between control and autonomy.

The task of the head is twofold: to administer the school in a way which optimises this balance and to provide professional leadership. The first of these tasks is exercised in different ways according to leadership style. The literature on educational leadership suggests that the most effective strategy is one which ensures that tasks are achieved and good social relationships are maintained. Within this strategy different styles can achieve the same result. However, leadership theory suggests that the most effective head is the one who can adopt a contingent style which involves variation according to circumstances. Moreover, there is a hierarchy whereby leadership transcends immediate organisational imperatives to conceptualise and transmit a less proximate set of organisational ends: from management to administration in Hodgkinson's terms.

Thus the task of the head is to work with colleagues to create a mission for the school. This is a difficult enterprise not only because some tasks for the school are imposed by external forces, but also because although there is scope for identifying a distinctive mission for a school, this must be related to a set of goals which is diverse, diffuse, long term, and not easily evaluated. There is the ever-present problem of organisational pathos, the gap between aspiration and achievement. The head-as-leader can overcome to some degree the centrifugal nature of the school by conceptualising, almost embodying, a mission with which teachers can identify and which will influence their professional practice. But there are many dangers here. The head who embodies a mission to a point of megalomania is unlikely to motivate teachers, although there are cases of heads who convert their colleagues into zealots but fail because their mission is rejected by the outside world. There are others who have succeeded in converting only a proportion of the staff and hence generating conflict. We know very little, in fact, about how heads work more unobtrusively to create 'modest' missions which are motivating and do not decline into bathos.

In matters of organisation and leadership, schools are unlike many other kinds of organisation. All organisations display epistemological, cognitive and logical limits to the operation of rationality, and schools are no exception. Moreover, schools are organisations in which symbols, as manifest in language, actions and artefacts, are particularly potent at many levels, not least at the managerial level. Thus management is much concerned with the symbolic construction of meaning especially in the relative absence of formal and explicit procedures. Meaning has to be construed from a complexity of signs, and can easily be misconstrued.

All organisations are characterised by micropolitics. Schools are no exception. The loosely-coupled structure of the school invites micropolitical activity since, although the head has a high degree of authority and responsibility, the relative autonomy of teachers and the norms of the teaching profession, serve to limit the pervasiveness and scope of this power. Moreover, although schools are not wholly collegial, a certain commitment to participation in decision-making remains following the sociopolitical trends of the 1960s. Thus heads frequently have recourse to micropolitical strategies in order to have their way. But teachers, too, are not without micropolitical resources. The problem with micropolitics is a moral one which raises age-old problems of ends and means. Micro-politics are inevitable, and may be morally acceptable in relation to their ends, but there are forms of self-interested, manipulative micropolitics which cannot easily be legitimated. This variety of micropolitics would be minimised by the professional development of teachers.

This further professional development of teachers which leads to their being better informed in relation to matters of policy, curriculum and management should enhance the quality of schools not only in relation to the process of schooling but also the quality of schools as organisations. There are signs that this is occurring as teachers and heads together are confronting the purposes of the school, the skills and resources needed to achieve these purposes, and how the attainment of these purposes might be evaluated by the school itself.

Bibliography

ABELL, PETER (ed) (1975) *Organizations as Bargaining and Influence Systems.* London: Heinemann.

ALLISON, G. T. (1971) *Essence of decision: Explaining the Cuban missile crisis.* Boston: Little, Brown & Co.

ALUTTO, JOSEPH A. and BELASCO, JAMES A. (1972) 'A typology for participation in organizational decision making', *Administrative Science Quarterly,* 17.

ANDERSON, J. G. (1967) 'The authority structure of the school: system of social exchange', *Educational Administration Quarterly,* 3(2).

ANDERSON, J. G. (1968) *Bureaucracy in Education.* Baltimore: Johns Hopkins University Press.

ARGYRIS, CHRIS (1957) *Personality and Organisation.* Harper: New York.

ARGYRIS, CHRIS (1964) *Integrating the Individual and the Organisation.* New York: Wiley.

AULD, R. (1976) *Report of the Public Inquiry into the William Tyndale junior and infant schools.* London: ILEA.

BACHARACH, P. and BARATZ, M. (1962) 'Two faces of power', *American Political Science Review,* 56.

BACHARACH, SAMUEL B. and LAWLER, EDWARD J. (1980) *Power and Politics in Organizations.* San Francisco: Jossey-Bass Inc.

BACHARACH, SAMUEL B. and LAWLER, EDWARD J. (1981) *Bargaining: Power, Tactics and Outcomes.* San Francisco: Jossey-Bass Inc.

BAILEY, A. J. (1981) *Patterns and Process of Change in Secondary Schools: a case study.* London: Social Science Research Council (unpublished).

BAILEY, A. J. (1982a) The question of legitimation: a response to Eric Hoyle, *Educational Management and Administration,* 10(2).

BAILEY, A. J. (1982b) *'The Patterns and Process of Change in Secondary Schools: a case study',* Unpublished PhD Thesis: University of Sussex.

BAILEY, F. G. (1965) 'Decisions by consensus in councils and committees' in BANTON, M. (ed) *Political Systems and the Distribution of Power.* London: Tavistock.

BAILEY, F. G. (1970) *Strategems and Spoils.* Oxford: Blackwell.

BAILEY, F. G. (1977) *Morality and Expediency: the Folklore of Academic Politics.* Oxford: Blackwell.

BALES, R. F. (1951) *Interaction Process Analysis.* Reading, Mass.: Addison-Wesley.

BALL, S. J. (1980) *Beachside Comprehensive.* Cambridge: Cambridge University Press.

BARLEY, S. R. (1983) 'Semiotics and the study of organizational and occupational cultures', *Administrative Science Quarterly*, 28.
BARNARD, Chester (1938) *Functions of the Executive*. Cambridge, Mass: Harvard University Press.
BASS, B. M. (1960) *Leadership, Psychology and Organizational Behaviour*, New York: Harper and Row.
BELL, L. A. (1980) 'The school as an organization', *British Journal of the Sociology of Education*, 1(2).
BENNIS, W. G. (1966) *Changing Organizations*. McGraw Hill: New York.
BENNETT, S. and WILKIE, R. (1973) 'Structural conflict in school organization' in FOWLER, G., MORRIS, V. and OZGA, T. (eds) *Decision-Making in Educational Administration*. London: Heinemann.
BERG, L. (1968) *Risinghill*. Harmondsworth: Penguin.
BERGER, P. L., BERGER, B. and KELLNER, H. (1974) *The Homeless Mind*. Harmondsworth: Penguin.
BERLACK, ANN and BERLACK, HAROLD (1981) *Dilemmas of Schooling*. New York: Methuen.
BERLIN, ISAIAH (1979) *Against the Current*. London: The Hogarth Press.
BERNBAUM, G. (1973) 'Countesthorpe College' in DALIN, P. (ed.) *Case Studies in Educational Innovation III: At the School Level*. Paris: OECD/CERI.
BERNSTEIN, BASIL (1967) 'Open schools, open society?', *New Society*, 10, 259.
BERNSTEIN, BASIL (1975) *Class, Codes and Control*, Vol. III. London: Routledge and Kegan Paul.
BIDWELL, C. E. (1965) 'The school as a formal organization' in MARCH, J. G. (ed.) *Handbook of Organizations*. Chicago: Rand McNally.
BLAU, P. M. (1964) *Exchange and Power in Social Life*. New York: Wiley.
BOLAM, RAY (1974) *Teachers as Innovators*. Paris: OECD.
BOLAM, RAY (ed.) (1982) *School-focused In-service Training*. London: Heinemann.
BORMANN, ERNEST, G. (1983) 'Symbolic convergence: organizational communication and culture' in PUTNAM, LINDA L. and PACANOWSKY, MICHAEL E. (eds.) *Communication in Organizations: an Interpretive Approach*. New York: Sage Publications.
BOWLES, S. and GINTIS, H. (1976) *Schooling in Capitalist America*. London: Routledge and Kegan Paul.
BRAYBROOKE, D. and LINDBLOM, C. E. (1963) *A Strategy of Decision*. New York: Free Press.
BRIMER, ALAN et al. (1977) *Sources of Differences in School Achievement*. New York: Carnegie Corporation.
BROWN, A. F. (1967) 'Reactions to leadership', *Educational Administration Quarterly*, 3.

BUCKLEY, W. (1967) *Sociology and Modern Systems Theory*. Englewood Cliffs, N. J.: Prentice-Hall.

BURNS, TOM (1955) 'The reference of conduct in small groups', *Human Relations*, 8.

BURNS, TOM (1961) 'Micropolitics: mechanisms of institutional change', *Administrative Science Quarterly*, 6 (3).

BURNS, T. and STALKER, G. M. (1961) *The Management of Innovation*. London: Tavistock.

BURRELL, GIBSON and MORGAN, GARETH (1979) *Sociological Paradigms and Organizational Analysis*. London: Heinemann.

CARLSON, D. (1984) 'Environmental constraints and educational consequences: the public schools and its clients' in GRIFFITHS, D. E. (ed.) *Behavioural Science and Educational Administration* (63rd NSSE Yearbook). Chicago: University of Chicago Press.

CASTLE, BARBARA (1980) *The Castle Diaries 1974-1976*. London: Weidenfeld and Nicolson.

CHAPIN, F. STUART (1935) *Contemporary American Institutions*. New York: Harper and Row.

CHRISTENSEN, S. (1976) 'Decision-making and socialization' in MARCH, J. G. and OLSEN, J. P. *Ambiguity and Choice in Organizations*.

CLARK, B. R. (1960) *The Open Door College*. New York: McGraw Hill.

CLARK, D. L. (1972) 'The organizational saga in higher education', *Administrative Science Quarterly*, 17.

COLEMAN, J. S. (1961) *The Adolescent Society*. New York: Free Press.

COLEMAN, J. S. et al. (1966) *Report on Equality of Educational Opportunity*. Washington: US Government Printing Office.

CONWAY, JAMES A. (1978) Power and participatory decision-making in selected English schools, *Journal of Educational Administration*, 16(1).

CORNFORD, F. M. (1973) *Microcosmographia Academia*. London: Bowes and Bowes (9th impression).

CORWIN, R. G. (1965) *A Sociology of Education*. New York: Appleton-Century-Croft.

CORWIN, R. G. (1970) *Militant Professionals: A Study of Organizational Conflict in High Schools*. New York: Appleton-Century-Croft.

CROSSMAN, RICHARD (1975) *The Diaries of a Cabinet Minister Vol. I: Minister of Housing 1964-6*. London: Hamish Hamilton/Cape.

CROSSMAN, RICHARD (1977) *The Diaries of a Cabinet Minister Vol. II: Lord President of the Council and Leader of the House 1966-8*. London: Hamish Hamilton/Cape.

CROZIER, Michel (1964) *The Bureaucratic Phenomenon*. London: Tavistock.

CROZIER, Michel (1975) 'Comparing structures and comparing games' in HOTSTEDE, G. and KASSEM, M. S. *European Contributions to Organization Theory* Assen: Van Gorcum. Reprinted in LOCKETT, MARTIN and SPEAR, ROGER (1980) *Organizations as Systems*. Milton Keynes: Open University Press.

DAHL, and LINDBLOM, C. E. (1953) *Politics, Economics and Welfare*. New York: Harper and Row.
DALIN, PER (1973) *Case Studies of Educational Innovation IV: Strategies for Innovation in Education*. Paris: OECD/CERI.
DALIN, PER and RUST, VAL D. (1983) *Can Schools Learn?* London: NFER/Nelson.
DAVIES, BRIAN (1971) 'On the contribution of organisational analysis to the study of educational institutions' in BROWN, R. (ed). *Knowledge, Education and Cultural Change*. London: Tavistock.
DAVIES, BRIAN (1982) 'Organizational theory and schools' in HARTNETT, A. (ed) *The Social Sciences in Educational Studies*. London: Heinemann.
DAVIES, HUNTER (1976) *The Creighton Report: A Year in the Life of a Comprehensive School*. London: Hamish Hamilton.
DAWSON, S. (1975) 'Power and influence in prison workshops' in ABELL, P. (ed) *Organizations as Bargaining and Influence Systems*. London: Heinemann.
DEPARTMENT OF EDUCATION AND SCIENCE (1977) *Education in Schools: A Consultative Document*. Cmnd 6869. London: HMSO.
DERR, BROOKLYN and GABARRO, JOHN (1972) 'An organizational contingency theory for education', *Educational Administration Quarterly*, 8.
DILL, W. R. (1964) 'Decision-making' in GRIFFITHS, D. E. (ed) *Behavioural Science and Educational Administration*. 63rd Yearbook of the National Society for the Study of Education. Chicago: University of Chicago Press.
DREEBEN, R. (1968) *On What is Learned in School*. New York: Addison-Wesley.
DREEBEN, R. (1976) 'The organizational structure of schools and school systems' in LOUBSER, JAN et al. (eds) *Explorations in General Theory in Social Sciences: Essays in Honor of Talcott Parsons*. New York: Free Press.
ELLIS, T. et al. (1976) *William Tyndale: The Teachers' Story*. London: Writers and Readers Co-operative.
ELSTER, Jon (1978) *Logic and Society*. New York: Wiley.
ELSTER, Jon (1979) *Ullysees and the Siren*, Cambridge: Cambridge University Press.
EMERY, F. E. and TRIST, E. L. (1972) *Towards a Social Ecology*. Harmondsworth: Penguin.
ETZIONI, A. (1975) *A Comparative Analysis of Complex Organizations* (rev. ed.). New York: Free Press.
FIEDLER, FRED (1965) 'Engineer the job to fit the manager', *Harvard Business Review* Sept-Oct.
FIEDLER, FRED E. and CHEMERS, M. M. (1974) *Leadership and Effective Management*. Glenview, Illinois: Scott, Foresman and Co.
FORD, J. (1969) *Social Class and the Comprehensive School*. London: Routledge and Kegan Paul.

FULLAN, M. (1972) 'Overview of the innovative process and the user', *Interchange*, 3.
FULLAN, M. (1982) *The Meaning of Educational Change*. Toronto: OISE Press.
GETZELS, J. W. and GUBA, E. G. (1957) 'Social behaviour and the administrative process', *School Review*. 65 Winter.
GILBERT, V. (1979) *Factors Influencing the Innovativeness of a Comprehensive School*. Unpublished PhD thesis, University of Bristol.
GIBSON, R. (1977) 'Bernstein's classification and framing', *Higher Education Review*, 9.
GLASER, B. and STRAUSS, A. (1967) *The Discovery of Grounded Theory*. London: Weidenfeld and Nicolson.
GLATTER, Ron (1982) 'The micropolitics of education:implications for training', *Educational Management and Administration*, 10 (2).
GOFFMAN, Erving (1969) *Strategic Interaction*. Philadelphia: Philadelphia University Press.
GOFFMAN, Erving (1971) *Relations in Public: Microstudies of the Public Order*. New York: Basic Books.
GOFFMAN, Erving (1974) *Frame Analysis – an Essay on the Organization of Experience*. New York: Harper and Row.
GORDON, C. V. (1957) *The Social System of the High School*. New York: Free Press.
GOULDNER, A. W. (1959) 'Organizational analysis' in MERTON, R. K., BROOM, L. and COTTRELL, L. S. (eds) *Sociology Today: Problems and prospects*. New York: Harper and Row.
GREENFIELD, THOMAS B. (1975) 'Theory about organizations: its implications for Schools' in HUGHES. M. (ed) *Administering Education: International Challenge*. London: Athlone Press.
GREENFIELD, THOMAS B. (1980) 'The man who comes back through the door in the wall: discovering truth, discovering self, discovering organizations', *Educational Administration Quarterly*, 16(3) Fall 1980.
GRETTON, J. and JACKSON, M. (1976) *William Tyndale: Collapse of a School – or a system?*. London: Allen and Unwin.
GRONN, PETER C. (1983) *Rethinking Educational Administration: T. B. Greenfield and his Critics* (ESA 841 Theory and Practice in Educational Administration). Geelong, Victoria: Deakin University.
GRONN, PETER C. (1984a) 'On studying administrators at work', *Educational Administration Quarterly*, 20 (1).
GRONN, PETER C. (1984b) 'I have a solution . . . .': Administrative power in a school meeting, *Educational Administration Quarterly*, 20(2).
GRONN, PETER C. (1985) 'Committee talk: negotiating personnel development at a training college', *Journal of Management Studies*, 22(3).
GROSS, EDWARD (1969) 'The definition of organizational goals', *British Journal of Sociology*, 20.

GROSS, N., GIACQUINTA, J. B. and BERNSTEIN, M. (1971) *Implementing Organizational Innovations*. New York: Harper and Row.
HALL, G. E. *et al.* (1982) 'Three change-facilitator styles'. Paper presented at the annual meeting of AERA, New York, 1982.
HALL, RICHARD H. (1963) 'The concept of bureaucracy: an empirical assessment', *American Journal of Sociology*, 69 No. 1.
HALPIN, ANDREW (1966) *Theory and Research in Administration*, New York: Macmillan.
HANDY, CHARLES B. (1976) *Understanding Organizations*. Harmondsworth: Penguin.
HANSON, E. MARK (1976) 'The profession-bureaucratic interface: a case study', *Urban Education*, 11(3).
HANSON, E. MARK (1979a) *Educational Administration and Organizational Behaviour*. Boston: Allyn and Bacon.
HANSON, E. MARK (1979b) 'School management and contingency theory: an emerging perspective', *Educational Administration Quarterly*, 15(2).
HANSON, E. MARK and BROWN, MICHAEL E. (1977) 'A contingency view of problem solving in schools: a case analysis', *Educational Administration Quarterly*, 13.
HARGREAVES, D. H. (1967) *Social Relations in a Secondary School*. London: Routledge and Kegan Paul.
HARGREAVES, D. H., HESTER, S. K. and MELLOR. F. J. (1975) *Deviance in Classrooms*. London: Routledge and Kegan Paul.
HAVELOCK, R. G. (1973) *The Change Agent's Guide to Innovation in Education*. Englewood Cliffs, N. J.: Educational Technology Publications Ltd.
HEMPHILL, J. K. (1964) 'Personal variables and administrative styles' in GRIFFITHS, D. E. (ed) *Behavioural Science and Educational Administration* (64th Yearbook of NSSE). Chicago: Chicago University Press.
HEMPHILL, JOHN and COONS, ALVIN (1957) *Leader Behaviour: its Description and Measurement*. Columbus, Ohio: Ohio State University Press.
HERRIOTT, ROBERT E. and FIRESTONE. WILLIAM A. (1984) 'Two images of schools as organizations: a refinement and elaboration', *Educational Administration Quarterly*, 20(4).
HEWARD, CHRISTINE (1975) *Bureaucracy and Innovation in Schools* Unpublished PhD, University of Birmingham.
HILLS, R. J. (1968) *Toward a Theory of Organisation*. Eugene, Oregon: Centre for the Advanced Study of Educational Administration.
HILLS, R. J. (1976) 'The public school as a type of organization' in LOUBSER, JAN *et al.* (eds) *Explorations in General Theory in Social Science: Essays in Honor of Talcott Parsons*. New York: Free Press.
HIRSCHMAN, A. O. (1978) *Exit, Voice and Loyalty*. Cambridge, Mass.: Harvard University Press.

HIRSCHMAN, A. O. (1981) *Essays in Trespassing: Economic Politics and Beyond.* Cambridge: Cambridge University Press.
HODGKINSON, C. (1953) *The Philosophy of Leadership.* Oxford: Blackwell.
HOFFER, E. (1951) *The true believer.* New York: Harper and Row.
HOMANS, G. C. (1958) 'Human behaviour as exchange' *American Journal of Sociology,* 63 (6).
HOMANS, G. C. (1961) *Social Behaviour: its Elementary Forms.* London: Routledge and Kegan Paul.
HOUSE, ROBERT (1971) 'A path-goal theory of leader effectiveness', *Administrative Science Quarterly,* 16.
HOUSE, ROBERT and DESSLER, GARY (1974) 'The path-goal theory of leadership: some post hoc and a priori tests' in HUNT, JAMES and LARSON, LARS (eds) *Contingency Approaches to Leadership.* Carbondale, Illinois: Southern Illinois University Press.
HOYLE, ERIC (1965) 'Organizational analysis in the field of education', *Educational Research,* 7(2).
HOYLE, ERIC (1969a) 'Professional stratification and anomie in the teaching profession', Pedagogica Europaea Vol. 5, *The Changing Role of the Professional Educator.* Elsevier: Amsterdam.
HOYLE, ERIC (1969b) 'Organizational theory and educational administration' in BARON, G. and TAYLOR, W. *Educational Administration and the Social Sciences.* London: Athlone Press.
HOYLE, ERIC (1970) 'Planned organizational change in education' *Research in Education,* 3. Reprinted in HARRIS, A., LAWN, M. and PRESCOTT, W. (eds) *Curriculum Innovation.* Windsor: Croom Helm.
HOYLE, ERIC (1973) 'The study of schools as organizations' in BUTCHER, H. J., and PONT, H. (eds) *Educational Research in Britain III.* London: University of London Press.
HOYLE, ERIC (1974) 'Professionality, professionalism and control in teaching', *London Educational Review* 3(2).
HOYLE, ERIC (1976a) 'Innovation and the school' in *Curriculum Design and Development,* Unit 29. Bletchley: Open University Press.
HOYLE, ERIC (1976b) 'Barr Greenfield and organization theory: a comment', *Educational Administration,* 5(1).
HOYLE, ERIC (1980) 'Professionalization and de-professionalization in education' in HOYLE, E. and MEGARRY, J. (eds) *World Yearbook of Education 1980: The Professional Development of Teachers.* London: Kogan Page.
HOYLE, ERIC (1981) 'The process of management' in *Management and the School* E 323 Block 3. Milton Keynes: Open University Press.
HOYLE, ERIC (1982) 'Micropolitics of educational organizations', *Educational Management and Administration,* 10 (2).
HOYLE, ERIC and McCORMICK, R. (1976) *Innovation and the School,* Open University Course E 203 Curriculum Design and Development Unit 29. Milton Keynes: Open University Press.

HUGHES, M. (1973) 'The professional as administrator: The case of the secondary school head', *Educational Administration Bulletin*, 2(1).
ILLICH, IVAN D. (1971) *Deschooling Society*. London: Calder.
JACKSON, PHILIP W. (1968) *Life in Classrooms*. New York: Holt, Rinehart and Winston.
JAEGER, GERTRUDE and SELZNICK, PHILIP (1964) 'A normative theory of culture', *American Sociological Review*, 29.
JANOWITZ, M. (1969) *Institution Building in Urban Education*. New York: Russell Sage.
KATZ, F. E. (1964) 'The school as a complex organization', *Harvard Educational Review*, 34.
KING, R. A. (1969) *Values and Involvement in a Grammar School*. London: Routledge and Kegan Paul.
KING, R. A. (1973) *School Organization and Pupil Involvement*. London: Routledge and Kegan Paul.
KING, R. A. (1976) 'Bernstein's Sociology of the School – some propositions tested', *British Journal of Sociology*, 27 (4).
KING, R. A. (1981) 'Bernstein's sociology of the school: a further testing', *British Journal of Sociology*, 2(2).
KING, R. A. (1983) *The Sociology of School Organization*. London: Routledge and Kegan Paul.
KLAPP, O. E. (1969) *Collective Search for Identity*. New York: Holt, Rinehart and Winston.
KOGAN, M. (1975) *Educational Policy Making*. London: Allen and Unwin.
LACEY, COLIN (1970) *Hightown Grammar*. Manchester: Manchester University Press.
LAMBERT, R, BULLOCK, R., and MILLHAM, J. (1973) 'The informal social system: an example of the limitations of organizational analysis' in BROWN, R. (ed) *Knowledge, Education and Cultural Change*. London: Tavistock.
LAMBERT, R. J. and MILLHAM, S. (1968) *The Hothouse Society*. London: Weidenfeld and Nicolson.
LAVER, MICHAEL (1981) *The Politics of Private Desires*. Harmondsworth: Penguin.
LAWRENCE, P. R. and LORSCH, J. W. (1967) *Organization and Environment*. Cambridge, Mass.: Harvard Graduate School of Business Administration.
LEITHWOOD, K. and MONTGOMERY, D. J. (1984) 'Patterns of growth in principal effectiveness'. Paper presented at the Annual Meeting of AERA, New Orleans, April, 1984.
LIKERT, R. (1961) *New Patterns of Managemnt*. New York: McGraw-Hill.
LINDBLOM, C. E. (1959) 'The science of muddling through', *Public Administration Review*, 19.
LINDBLOM, C. E. (1966) *The Intelligence of Democracy*. New York: Free Press.

LINDBLOM, C. E. (1968) *The Policy Making Process*. Englewood Cliffs, N. J.: Prentice Hall.

LITWAK, E. (1961) 'Models of bureaucracy which permit conflict', *American Journal of Sociology*, 67.

LITWAK, E. and MEYER, M. J. (1965) 'Administrative styles and community linkages of public schools' in REISS, A. J. (ed) *Schools in a Changing Society*. New York: Free Press.

LITWAK, E. and MEYER, H. J. (1974) *School, Family and Neighbourhood*. New York: Columbia University Press.

LORTIE, D. C. (1964) 'The teacher and team teaching' in SHAPLIN, J. J. and OLDS, H. (eds) *Team Teaching*. New York: Harper and Row.

LORTIE, D. C. (1969) 'The balance of control and autonomy in elementary school teaching' in ETZIONI A. (ed) *The Semi-Professions and their Organisations*. New York: Free Press.

LORTIE, D. C. (1975) *Schoolteacher – a sociological study*. Chicago: University of Chicago Press.

LOUIS, K. S. and SIEBER, S. (1979) *Bureaucracy and the Dispersed Organization*. Norwood, N. J.: Ablex Publishing Corporation.

McGREGOR, D. M. (1960) *The Human side of Enterprise*. New York: McGraw-Hill.

McHUGH, ROYSTON (1976) 'A case study in management: Sidney Stringer School and Community College', Open University Course E 321: *Management in Education* Unit 2. Milton Keynes: Open University.

McKENZIE, R. (1970) *State School*. Penguin.

McMAHON, Agnes (1986) 'The self evaluation of schools' in HOYLE, E. and McMAHON, A. (eds) *World Yearbook of Education, 1986: The Management of Schools*. London: Kogan Page.

McMULLEN, T. (1968) 'Flexibility for a comprehensive school', *Forum*, 10 (2).

MANGHAM, IAIN (1978) *Interactions and Interventions*. New York: Wiley.

MANGHAM, IAIN (1979) *The Politics of Organizational Change*. London: Associated Business Press.

MARCH, J. G. and SIMON, HERBERT A. (1958) *Organisations*. New York: Wiley.

MARCH, J. G. and OLSEN, J. P. (1976) (eds) *Ambiguity and Choice in Organization*. Bergen: Universitetforlaget.

MARLAND, MICHAEL (1982) 'The politics of improvement in schools', *Educational Management and Administration*, 10(2).

MARTIN, WILLIAM J. and WILLOWER, DONALD (1981) 'The managerial behaviour of high school principals', *Educational Administration Quarterly*, 17.

MAYO, ELTON (1933) *The Human Problems of an Industrial Civilization*. New York: Macmillan.

MEAD, G. H. (1934) *Mind, Self and Society*. Chicago: University of Chicago Press.
MERTON, ROBERT (1958) *Social Theory and Social Structure* (rev. ed.). New York: Free Press.
MILES, M. B. (1965) 'Planned change and organizational health' in CARLSON, R. et al. *Change Processes in the Public Schools*. Eugene, Oregon: University of Oregon, Centre for Advanced Study of Educational Administration.
MILLER, E. J. and RICE, P. K. (1967) *Systems and Organization*. London: Tavistock.
MOELLER, G. H. and CHARTERS, W. W. (1966) 'The relation of bureaucratisation to a sense of power among teachers', *Administrative Science Quarterly*, 10.
MORGAN, G. (1980) Paradigms, metaphors and puzzle solving in organisational theory, *Administrative Science Quarterly*, Vol. (4).
MURRAY, DOMINIC (1983) *A Comparative Study of the Culture and Character of Protestant and Catholic Primary Schools in Northern Ireland*. Unpublished PhD thesis: New University of Ulster.
MUSGROVE, FRANK (1971) *Patterns of Power and Authority in English Education*. London: Methuen.
NIAS, J. (1980) 'Leadership styles and job satisfaction in primary schools' in BUSH, T. et al. (ed) *Approaches to School Management*. London: Harper and Row/Oxford University Press.
NOBLE, T. and PYM, B. (1970) 'Collegial authority and the receding locus of power', *British Journal of Sociology*, 21(4).
O'DEMPSEY, KEITH (1976) 'The analysis of work-patterns and roles of high school principals', *Administrator's Bulletin*, 7(8).
OLSON, M. (1965) *The logic of Collective Action*. Cambridge, Mass.: Harvard University Press.
PACKWOOD, TIM (1977) 'Hierarchy, anarchy and accountability: contrasting perspectives', *Educational Administration*, 5 (2).
PARSONS, T. (1951) *The Social System*. New York: Free Press.
PARSONS, T. (1959) 'The school class as a social system', *Harvard Educational Review*, 29.
PARSONS, T. (1966) 'Some ingredients of a general theory of organization' in HALPIN, A. W. (ed) *Administrative Theory in Education*. Chicago: University of Chicago Press.
PARSONS, T. and BALES, R. F. (eds) (1955) *Family, Socialization and Interaction Process*. Glencoe: Free Press.
PERROW, CHARLES (1961) 'The analysis of goals in complex organisations', *American Sociological Review*, Vol. 26.
PERROW, CHARLES (1968) 'Organizational goals' in *International Encyclopaedia of the Social Sciences*. London: Macmillan.
PERROW, CHARLES (1972a) *Organizational Analysis: a Sociological View*. London: Tavistock.

PERROW, CHARLES (1972b) *Complex Organisations: a critical essay.* Glenview, Illinois: Scott, Foresman and Co.
PFEFFER, JEFFREY (1981a) *Power in Organizations.* Marshfield, Mass.: Pitman.
PFEFFER, JEFFREY (1981b) 'Management as symbolic action: the creation and maintenance of organizational paradigms' in CUMMINGS, L. K. and SHAW, B. M. (eds) *Research on Organizational Behavior* Vol. III. Greenwich, CT: JAI Press.
PETERS, THOMAS J. (1978) 'Symbols, patterns and settings: an optimistic case for getting things done', *Organizational Dynamics,* 7(3).
PETERSON, K. (1976) 'The principal's tasks', *Administrator's Notebook,* 26(8).
PETTIGREW, A. M. (1972) 'Information control as a power resource', *Sociology,* 6(2).
PETTIGREW, A. M. (1973) *The Politics of Organizational Decision Making.* London: Tavistock.
PONDY, LOUIS, R. (1978) 'Leadership is a language game' in McCALL, M. W. and LOMBARDO, M. M. (eds) *Leadership: Where Else Can we Go?.* Durham, N C: Duke University Press.
POWER, M. J. *et al.* (1967) 'Schools for Delinquency?', *New Society,* 10, 264.
PRESCOTT, W. (ed) (1976) *Portrait of Countesthorpe College,* E 203 Curriculum Design and Development Case Study 5. Milton Keynes: Open University Press.
PUGH, D. S. and HININGS, C. R. (eds) (1976) *Organisational Structure, Extensions and Replications: The Aston Programme II.* Farnborough: Saxon House.
PUNCH, K. F. (1969) 'Bureaucratic structure in schools: towards redefinition and measurement', *Educational Administration Quarterly,* 5(2).
RAPAPORT, A. (1966) *The Person Game Theory.* Ann Arbor: University of Michigan Press.
RAYNOR, JOHN *et al.* (1974) *The Educative Community,* Course E 351 Urban Education, Block 4. Milton Keynes: Open University Press.
REDDIN, W. J. (1970) *Managerial Effectiveness.* New York: McGraw-Hill.
REVANS, R. W. (1965) 'Involvement in school', *New Society,* 6, 152.
REYNOLDS, D. and SULLIVAN, M. (1979) 'Bringing schools back in' in BARTON, L. and MEIGHAN, R. (eds) *Schools, Pupils and Deviance.* Driffield: Nafferton Books.
RICHARDSON, E. (1973) *The Teacher, the School and the task of Management.* London: Heinemann.
ROKKAN, STEIN (1968) 'Norway: Numerical Democracy and Corporate Pluralism' in DAHL, R. A. (ed) *Political Opportunities in Western Democracies.* New Haven: Yale University Press.
ROETHLSBERGER, F. I. and DICKSON, W. J. (1939) *Management and the Worker.* Cambridge, Mass.: Harvard University Press.

RUTTER, M. *et al.* (1979) *Fifteen Thousand Hours: Secondary Schools and their Effects on Children*. London: Open Books.
SCHMUCK, RICHARD A. *et al. Second Handbook of Organizational Development in Schools*. Palo Alto, Cal.: Mayfield Publishing Co.
SCHMUCK, RICHARD A. and MILES, MATTHEW B. (1971) *Organizational Development in Schools*. Palo Alto, Cal.: Mayfield Publishing Co.
SCHON, D. (1971) *Beyond the Stable State*. Harmondsworth: Penguin.
SELZNICK, P. (1957) *Leadership in Administration*. New York: Harper and Row.
SHARP, R. and GREEN, A. G. (1976) *Education and Social Control*. London: Routledge and Kegan Paul.
SILLS, D. L. (1957) *The Volunteers*. New York: Free Press.
SIMON, H. (1964) *Administrative Behaviour: a Study of Decision Making Processes in Administrative organization* (2nd ed.). New York: Collier Macmillan.
SKIDMORE, WILLIAM (1975) *Theoretical Thinking in Sociology*. Cambridge: Cambridge University Press.
SMIRCICH, L. and MORGAN, G. (1982) 'Leadership: the management of meaning', *Journal of Applied Behavioural Science*, 18.
SMITH, L. and KEITH, P. (1971) *Anatomy of Educational Innovation: an Organizational Analysis of an Elementary School*. New York: Wiley.
SPROULL, LEE S (1981) 'Managing educational programs: a microbehavioural analysis', *Human Organization*, 40.
STOGDILL, RALPH (1948) 'Personal factors associated with leadership', *Journal of Psychology*, 25.
STRAUSS, ANSELM *et al.* (1963) 'The hospital and its negotiated order' in FREIDSON, ELIOT (ed) *The Hospital in Modern Society*. New York: Free Press.
SWIDLER, ANNE (1979) *Organization without Authority*. Cambridge, Mass.: Harvard University Press.
SYKES, G. M. (1956) 'The conception of authority and reconciliation', *Social Forces*, 34.
TANNENBAUM, R. and SCHMIDT, W. H. (1958) 'How to choose a leadership pattern', *Harvard Business Review*, 51(3).
TANNENBAUM, ROBERT, WEISCHLER, I. and MASSARIK, F. (1961) *Leadership and Organization: a Behavioural Science Approach*. Urbana, Illinois: University of Illinois Press.
TAYLOR, CHARLES (1985) 'Interpretation and the sciences of man' in *Philosophical Papers*, Vol. 2. Cambridge: Cambridge University Press.
THIBAUT, JOHN and KELLEY, HAROLD (1959) *The Social Psychology of Groups*. New York: Wiley.
TYLER, WILLIAM (1973) 'The organizational structure of the secondary school' *Educational Review*, 25(3).
TYLER, WILLIAM (1982) *The Sociology of the School: A Review*. Herne Bay: William Tyler.
TYLER, WILLIAM (1983) 'Organizations, factors and codes: a meth-

odological enquiry into Bernstein's theory of educational transmissions'. Unpublished PhD thesis, University of Kent.

URBAN, GEORGE (1981) 'The perils of foreign policy: a conversation with Dr Zbigniew Brezinski', *Encounter*, May (98).

VON NEUMANN, K. and MORGENSTERN, O. (1944) *Theory of Games and Economic Behaviour*. Princeton, N. J.: Princeton University Press.

WAKEFORD, J. (1969) *The Cloistered Elite*. London: Macmillan.

WALLER, WILLARD (1932) *The Sociology of Teaching*. New York: Wiley.

WATTS, J.(ed) (1977) *The Countesthorpe Experience*. London: Allen and Unwin.

WEBER, M. (1947) *The Theory of Social and Economic Organisation* (trans. A. Henderson and T. Parsons). New York: Free Press.

WEICK, KARL (1970) 'Educational organizations as loosely-coupled systems', *Educational Administrative Quarterly*, 21.

WELDY, G. R. (1979) *Principals: What they Do and Who they Are*. Reston, Virginia: National Association of Secondary School Principals.

WHITTY, GEOFF (1974) 'Sociology and the problem of radical educational change' in FLUDE, M. and AHIER, J. (eds) *Educability, Schools and Ideology*. London: Croom Helm.

WHITESIDE, TOM (1978) *The Sociology of Educational Innovation*. London: Methuen.

WILLIS, QUENTIN (1980) 'The work activity of school principals: an observational study', *Journal of Educational Administration*, 18.

WILLOWER, D. T. (1980) 'Contemporary issues in theory in educational administration', *Educational Administration Quarterly*, 16 (3).

WILLOWER, D. J. (1982) 'School organizations: perspectives in juxtaposition'. *Educational Administration Quarterly*, 18 (3).

WILLOWER, D. J. (1983) 'Analogies gone awry: replies to Hill and Gronn', *Educational Administration Quarterly*, 19 (1).

WOOLCOTT, HARRY (1973) *The Man in the Principal's Office*. New York: Holt, Rinehart and Winston.

WOODS, P. (1979) *The Divided School*. London: Routledge and Kegan Paul.

WOODS, P. and HAMMERSLEY, M. (eds) (1977) *School Experience*. London: Croom Helm.

WOODWARD, J. (1965) *Industrial Organisation, Theory and Practice*. Oxford: Oxford University Press.

WOODWARD, J. (1972) *Industrial Organisation: Behaviour and Control*. Oxford: Oxford University Press.

YUKL, G. (1975) 'Towards a behavioural theory of leadership' in HOUGHTON, V. et al. (ed) *The Management of Organizations and Individuals*. London: Ward Lock.

ZALEZNIK, A (1966) *Human Dilemmas of Leadership*. New York: Harper and Row.

Index

Abell, Peter 131-2, 138
adaptive systems model, 38
administration, 114, 119
administrative man, 62
aggregation model, 35
Allison, G. T., 71
aloofness, 107
Alutto, Joseph A., 92
Anderson, J. G., 28, 139
Argyris, Chris, 106
Arnold, Thomas, 118
association, 161
Auld, R., 45, 97
authority, 73-91, 129
autocrats, 106
autonomous climate, 108
autonomy, 36, 38, 58, 84-85

Bacharach, P., 146
Bacharach, Samuel B., 73-9, 129, 132-3
Bailey, A. J., 70, 135, 149
Bailey, F. G., 143-4, 164
Bales, R. F., 8
Ball, S. J., 15
Baratz, M., 146
bargaining, 130-2, 133, 144
Barnard, Chester, 106
Bass, B. M., 106
Belasco, James A., 92
Bell, L. A., 16
Bennett, S., 142
Bennis, W. G., 38
Berg, L., 122
Berger, B., 25
Berger, P. L., 25
Berlack, Ann, 35
Berlack, Harold, 35
Berlin, Isaiah, 70-71
Bernbaum, G., 45
Bernstein, B., 17, 34-6, 37, 45, 151
Bernstein, M., 19
Bidwell, C. E., 22
Blau, P. M., 130, 131
Bolam, Ray, 47, 102
Bormann, Ernest G., 159
boundary, 35
Bowles, S., 16
Braybrooke, D., 63
Brimer, Alan, 20
Brown, A. F., 106
Brown, M. E., 42, 44
Brzezinski, Zbigniew, 71
Buckley, W., 7
Bullock, R., 15
bureaucracy, 23-33, 39, 49, 90
bureaucratic personality type, 24
bureaucratic-professional conflict, 79-85
Burns, Tom, 27, 38, 42, 128
Burrell, Gibson, 1, 10, 43

cabals, 128

Cambire School, 47
Carlson, D., 63
Castle, Barbara, 125
Chapin, F. Stuart, 91
charisma, 99
Charters, W. W., 29
Christensen, S., 69, 70
Clark, B. R., 19, 59, 159
Clark, D. L., 159
classification, 17, 34
climate, 3, 6, 16, 108
cliques, 128
coalitions, 129
Coleman, J. S., 17, 20
collegial authority, 40, 86-91, 99-100
community mode meetings, 147
'community' as symbol, 156-7
compromisers, 106
conflict theory, 9-10
consensus, 8, 31, 48
consideration, 106, 108, 109
consultation, 91-3
contingency theory of leadership, 108-9
contingency theory of management, 43, 49-50
controlled climate, 108
control of information, 142
control of meetings, 143
Conway, James A., 92
co-optation, 141
coordination, 22-3, 27, 30, 169
Cornford, F. M., 143
Corwin, R. G., 68, 81, 83, 91
Countesthorpe College, 44-5, 85-97, 159, 160
Creighton School, 147-8
Crossman, Richard, 125
Crozier, Michel, 134
culture, 3, 150, 158
curriculum, 3, 35

Dahl, R., 63
Dalin, Per, 47, 102
Davies, Brian, 2, 19
Davies, Hunter, 147
Dawson, S., 132
decision-centralisation, 109, 110
decision-making, 65-8
Department of Education and Science, 57
Derr, Brooklyn, 43
Dessler, Gary, 108
developers, 116
Dickson, W. J., 26
differentiation, 43
Dill, W. R., 94
disengagement, 106
displacement, 141
dividing and ruling, 140
'documentation' as symbolic, 165-6
domesticated organisations, 63
Dreeben, R., 8

Duane, Michael, 122
Durkheim, E., 17, 34

Ellis, Terry, 97, 122
Elster, Jon, 64
equifinality, 7
equilibrium, 131
esprit, 107
Ethnic High School, 98–9
ethnomethodology, 10
Eton College, 150, 153, 154
Etzioni, A., 75
exchange theory, 130–1, 136–9, 144
expectations, 4

familiar climate, 108
Fiedler, Fred, 108
Firestone, William A., 32
Ford, J., 15
framing, 17, 34
Fullan, M., 47
functions, 8, 9

Gabarro, John, 44
games theory, 133
garbage-can model, 66–7
Gemeinschaft, 156–7
general systems theory, 7
Gesellschaft, 157
Getzels, J. W., 4, 108
Giacquinta, J. B., 19
Gilbert, V., 159
Gibson, R., 17, 34
Gintis, H., 16
Glaser, B., 19
Glatter, R., 149
goals, 1, 8, 9, 48, 51–60, 68–70, 110, 129, 170
Goffman, Erving, 133, 162
Gordon, C. V., 17
Gouldner, A. W., 10
Green, A. G., 45
Green Paper, 57
Greenfield, Thomas B., 10, 11, 12–13, 18
Gretton, J., 45
Gronn, Peter, 18, 102, 135, 143, 146, 158
Gross, Edward, 54, 55
Gross, Neil, 19, 47
group, 6, 108
Group High School, 98–9, 164
Guba, E. G., 4, 108

Hall, G. E., 110
Hall, Richard H., 26, 28
Halpin, Andrew, 92, 106–8, 109, 110
Hammersley, M., 151
Handy, Charles B., 127
Hanson, E. Mark, 42, 44, 106, 109
Hargreaves, D. H., 15, 151
Havelock, R. G., 47
headteachers, 73–100, 118–23, 170
Hemphill, J. K., 105
Herriott, Robert E., 32

Hester, S. K., 151
Heward, Christine, 29
hidden agendas, 125, 164
hierarchy, 24–6, 29, 40, 170
'Hillford' School, 159
Hills, R. J., 8
hindrance, 107
Hinings, C. R., 29
Hirschman, A. O., 64
Hodgkinson, C., 103–5, 114–15, 124
Hoffer, E., 160
holism, 16–18
Holroyde, Geoffrey, 156
Homans, G. C., 130, 131
homeostasis, 7
hourglass model, 20–1
House, Robert, 108
Hoyle, Eric, 2, 14, 19, 34, 47, 80, 81, 84, 87, 106, 120, 126, 135, 136, 143
Hughes, M., 119
human relations, 27, 38, 39, 49

ideal type 23–4
idiographic dimension, 4, 106
Illich, Ivan D., 18
impersonality, 24
influence, 73–91, 129, 132
informal structure, 3
initiating structure, 106, 109, 110
institution, 4
integration, 22–3, 27, 43, 169
interacting spheres model, 85–6
interaction, 6, 83
interests, 128, 129, 140
interest sets, 128
intimacy, 107
investment, 139

Jackson, M., 45
Jackson, Philip W., 37, 120
Jaeger, Gertrude, 153
Janowitz, M., 34
John, Denys, 95, 118–19

Katz, F. E., 28
Keith, P., 19, 45–6, 120, 156, 160
Kelley, Howard, 130
Kellner, H., 25
Kensington School, 45–6, 120, 156
King, R. A., 15, 17, 19, 34, 35, 36, 151
Klapp, O. E., 160
Kogan, M., 71

Lacey, Colin, 15
Lambert, R., 15
Laver, Michael, 133
Lawler, Edward J., 73–9, 129, 132–3
Lawrence, P. R., 43
Leader Behaviour Description Questionnaire, 106
leadership, 101–23, 102–16
leadership style, 94, 105–111
leadership styles:

authoritarian, 105
autocrat, 116
Bourbon, 109
careerist, 116–17
compromiser, 116
democratic, 105
developer, 116
laissez faire, 105
mediative, 116
missionary, 116
poet, 116–17
politician, 116
positive, 109
proactive, 116
reactive, 116
technician, 116
legitimacy, 129, 149
Leithwood, K., 110, 111
Likert, R., 106
Lindblom, C. E., 63
Litwak, E., 39, 40, 41
loosely-coupled systems, 22, 36, 38–44, 49, 169
Lortie, D. C., 36, 37, 86, 87
Louis, K. S., 8

McGregor, D. M., 27
Machiavellianism, 125
McHugh, Royston, 136
McKenzie, R., 122
McMahon, Agnes, 102
McMullen, Tim, 45, 96, 158
'management' as symbol, 157
Mangham, I., 18, 133–4
manipulation, 144–7
Mapledean Junior School, 16
March, James C., 62, 65–72, 134
Marland, Michael, 128, 142, 165
Martin, William J., 101
Marxism, 16
masks, 164–5
Massarik, F., 108
Mayo, Elton, 26
Mead, G. H., 151–2, 153
mediative leadership, 116
meetings, 143–4
meetings as symbolic, 163–4
Mellor, F. J., 151
Merton, Robert, 24
method of continuous comparison, 20
Meyer, M. J., 39, 40, 41
micropolitical strategies, 140–6
micropolitics, 125–149, 171
Miles, M. B., 47
militant professionalism, 83–4
Miller, E. J., 17
Millham, S., 15
mission, 101–23
mobilising support, 160
Model A schools, 32–6, 41–2, 48, 49
Model B schools, 32–6, 41–2, 48, 49
Model C schools, 41–2
Moeller, G. H., 29

Montgomery, D. J., 110, 111
Morgan, G., 1, 10, 43, 155
Morgenstern, O., 133
Murray, Dominic, 160
Musgrove, Frank, 40

Nailsea School, 95, 118–19, 155
needs, 4
negotiated order, 86
Neill, A. S., 59, 95, 118, 121
Nias, J., 109–10, 121
Noble, T., 90
nomethetic dimension, 4, 106

O'Dempsey, Keith, 101
Olsen, J. P., 65–72, 134
Olson, M., 64
open climate, 106
open schools, 34, 36–7, 44–8
open systems, 42, 63
optimising, 62
organic adaptive pattern, 27
organisation as:
  economic system, 18
  political system, 18
  social construct, 10–14, 18
  social system, 7–10, 12–16, 17
  socio-technical system, 17
  structure, 16–17
  symbol system, 17
  theatre, 17–18
organisation theory, 1–21, 53–4, 65, 112, 134
organisational ambiguity, 66
organisational character, 112
organisational choice, 16
organisational mode meetings, 147
organisational myth, 159–60
organisational pathos, 51–2, 60–1
organisational saga, 159
organised anarchy, 67–8
organismic pattern, 27, 38

Packwood, Tim, 29
Parsons, T., 8
participation in decision-making, 33, 91–9, 114, 135
participative pattern, 27
paternal climate, 106
path-goal theory of leadership, 108
pedagogy, 3, 35, 89
Perrow, C., 27, 53, 56, 112
person dimension, 105, 109
personality, 4
Peters, Richard, 37
Peters, Thomas J., 162–7
Peterson, K., 101
Pettigrew, A. M., 127, 134
Pfeffer, Jeffrey, 160
phenomenological perspective, 6, 10–16, 54
political studies of organisations, 134
Pondy, Louis R., 155

possibilitarianism, 47
power, 74–91
Power, M. J., 20
Prescott, W., 158
prime taks, 23
proactive leadership, 116
procedural rules, 24
process, 6, 14, 15, 95
production emphasis, 107
profession, 80
professional development, 171
professionalism, 84
professionality, 84, 120
professionals, 39, 58, 79–85, 119
Pugh, D. S., 29
Punch, K. F., 28
Pym, B., 90

quieting opposition, 160

Rapaport, A., 133
rationality, 60–5
Raynor, John, 41
Reddin, W. J., 116
reification, 10
relative deprivation, 136
restricted professionality, 120
Revans, R. W., 16
Reynolds, D., 20
rhetorical community, 159
Rice, P. K., 17
Richardson, E., 19, 95, 118–19, 195, 165–6
Risinghill School, 122
Roethlisberger, F. I., 26
Rokkan, Stein, 69
role, 4
roles as symbolic, 165–6
Rust, V., 102
Rutter, M., 16, 19, 20

satisficing, 66
Schmidt, W. H., 92–3, 108, 114
Schmuck, Richard A., 47
Schon, D., 63
Selznick, P., 112–13, 129, 153
Sharp, R., 45
Sidney Stringer School, 156
Sieber, S., 8
signs, 152–3
Sills, D. L., 68
'Silverwood' School, 86
Simmel, G., 64–5
Simon, H., 62
Skidmore, William, 131
Smircich, Linda, 155
Smith, L., 19, 45–6, 120, 156, 160
social construct, 10–14
social geography, 162
socialisation, 8, 9
social psychology of influence, 133
socio-technical systems, 7, 18

space as symbolic, 161–62
specialisation, 35
specialisation model, 24, 28, 32, 35
Sproull, Lee S., 101
Stalker, G. M., 27, 38, 42
Stogdill, Ralph, 105
Strauss, Anselm, 19, 86
structural functionalism, 8
structuralism, 17
structural looseness, 22, 31
structure, 3
Sullivan, M., 20
Summerhill, 59
support tasks, 23
Swidler, Anne, 19, 65, 98, 164
Sykes, G. M., 127
symbols, 151–67, 171
symbol as surrogate, 166
symbolic interactionism, 152
systems perspective, 7–10, 12–16

Tannenbaum, R., 92–3, 108, 114
task dimension, 105, 109
Taylor, C., 34
Taylor, F. M., 26, 102
technical competence, 29
Theory X, 27
Theory Y, 27
Thibaut, John, 130
thrust, 107
time as symbolic, 163
tokenism, 141
traditional authority, 31
transactional style of leadership, 108
Tyler, William, 17, 36, 41, 43

unions, 143, 147
Urban, George, 71

Von Neumann, K., 133

Wakeford, J., 151
Waller, Willard, 150
Watts, John, 45, 96–7
Weber, M., 15, 17, 23, 24, 31, 34, 73, 78
Weick, Karl, 22, 38–9, 48, 155
Weischler, I., 108
Whitty, Geoff, 47
Whiteside, Tom, 47
Wilby, Parker, 35
wild organisations, 63
Wilkie, R., 142
William Tyndale Junior School, 45, 47, 97–8, 122
Willis, Quentin, 101
Willower, D. T., 22, 101, 102
Woolcott, Harry, 101
Woods, P., 15, 120, 151
Woodward, J., 17

Yukl, G., 109, 110

Zaleznik, A., 116